TRAINING ESSENTIALS

MASTERING

INSTRUCTIONAL DESIGN

IN

TECHNOLOGY-BASED

TRAINING

Judith Christian-Carter

Chartered Institute of Personnel and Development

© Judith Christian-Carter 2001

First published in 2001

Design and typesetting by Paperweight
Printed in Great Britain by
The Cromwell Press, Wiltshire

British Library Cataloguing in Publication Data
A catalogue record for this book is available from the
British Library

ISBN
0-85292-874-2

Chartered Institute of Personnel and Development, CIPD House,
Camp Road, London SW19 4UX
Tel.: 020-8971 9000   Fax: 020-8263 3333
E-mail: cipd@cipd.co.uk   Website: www.cipd.co.uk
Incorporated by Royal Charter. Registered charity no. 1079797

Contents

This book is dedicated to two of my very best friends, Mick and Tara, without whose patience and understanding it would never have been written.

Preface

As far as I am concerned, the heart of producing high-quality technology-based training programmes lies not in whiz-bang graphics, snazzy programming or seductive voice-overs but in really good instructional design. This book sets out to show you what I think good instructional design is all about, and how it should be used when producing technology-based training programmes. If you want to undertake some instructional design yourself or need to know what to look for when commissioning or using technology-based training, then this book will go a long way to helping you. The emphasis is very much on the practical application of instructional design in relation to technology-based training. Taking you first through some important prerequisites I then go on to describe the various processes and procedures that lie behind producing well-designed and effective technology-based training programmes.

Judith Christian-Carter
Warwickshire, England

Acknowledgements

I would like to thank Jan Seabrook for all her excellent advice and constructive feedback, particularly when, having waded through the manuscript, she emerged on the other side still smiling and gave me the confidence to complete the job. My thanks also go to Anne Cordwent of the CIPD, who has been simply the best editor with whom I have ever worked.

1

The Power of Instructional Design

Introduction

Have you ever been on a course and experienced that 'eureka' moment which comes when, after you have been really struggling to get your head around something, it suddenly all becomes crystal clear? If you have, then it's likely that you have been on the receiving end of some good instructional design. But what about those times when you have sat and wondered what on earth was going on and whether you were living on a planet controlled by training aliens from the planet Enigma? Indeed, amongst other things, you might even have thought, 'Instructional design – what instructional design?'

Instructional design is the one aspect that really distinguishes good training from poor. You can provide training that is related to the needs of the organisation and that supports identified learning needs, just as you can build into any training provision all manner of 'bells and whistles', but unless the overall instructional design is good the outcome will be ineffective.

Instructional design underpins all training provision. It is all about the way in which training is structured and sequenced and then developed to support not only the needs of the organisation, but also the identified learning needs of staff and the learning objectives or outcomes. In addition, it needs to take into account the means by which the training is going to be delivered so that it makes the most of the selected media. Although there is no single form of instructional design, there are quite a few best-practice guidelines, and it is upon these that this book is based.

There is a lot more to instructional design than just taking into account the various ways in which people prefer to learn. As far as I am concerned, instructional design needs to:

■ be linked directly to what it is people need to learn, in terms of knowledge and skills

■ take every step to assist people in transferring their learning to workplace performance

■ support the learning benefits and features of the media by which the training will be delivered

■ take into account what is known about the target audience

■ relate to the ways in which adults learn.

This chapter will look in some detail at the issue of definitions, the reason instructional design is so important, and what constitutes best practice in relation to providing instructionally sound, cost-effective training solutions. It also provides an overall structure for the remainder of the book by setting out the basics of instructional design that need to be taken on board when producing technology-based training (TBT).

When I use a word...

Some people prefer not to use the term 'instructional design' because 'instruction' has specific connotations, in particular the image of an instructor standing behind a lectern and disseminating words of wisdom to an assembled mass of trainees who may be seen as 'empty vessels'. For these people a more suitable term is often used: 'learning design'.

However, even though training is a form of learning, 'instruction' is now the favoured term, chiefly because training tends to be instructional in nature, in that it is concerned with the specific knowledge and skills required by people for their workplace performance. The term 'design' also deserves an explanation. Training *design* starts, once learning needs have been identified in relation to an organisation's objectives, with the production of a 'blueprint' or instructional strategy. It is this strategy or blueprint that is then developed into a training solution. So, in the context of training, and because the term 'instructional design' is still commonly used to mean the same thing, it is this term that is used throughout this book, even though at its very heart lies the concept of learning.

Why instructional design is important

If people are to acquire and develop all the knowledge and skills they need in order to perform effectively in the workplace, then the process by which they learn these essential aspects must be given a high priority in the total scheme of things. Even as children, all of us learn effectively when we know what is expected of us and when what we need to learn is presented in such a way that it makes sense. As Milton observed in *Paradise Regain'd*:

> In them is plainest taught, and easiest learnt,
> What makes a nation happy, and keeps it so.

Can you think of something that you managed to learn relatively easily? If you can, then why exactly was it easy for you to learn it? For example, was it easy because it was something you already knew about, because of the way it was explained or shown to you, or because it was something that you really wanted to learn? Jot down the things that made this piece of learning easy for you.

The eureka factor

When, in Bernard Shaw's *Pygmalion*, Eliza Doolittle finally manages to enunciate correctly, 'The rain in Spain falls mainly on the plain', Professor Higgins is heard to say, 'By George, she's got it!' Indeed she had, and for her this could be described as a 'eureka' moment – provided, that is, she managed to pronounce 'er first two vowels correctly! When we say 'I've got it', it's often as a result of much trial and tribulation. I am not for one moment suggesting that the professor's instructional design was inadequate – after all, in Miss Doolittle he had taken on quite a challenge – but if everyone's learning was as gruelling as Eliza's, most of us would probably give it up as a bad show and stay in our present jobs, even if this meant selling flowers in Covent Garden for the rest of our lives!

Although learning can be likened to a voyage of discovery, most of us would prefer to travel first class and to achieve our destination in style. This is where instructional design comes in. With good instructional design we can all experience the 'eureka' factor many times over, with the minimum of stress and tribulation.

So what makes for good instructional design?

How was it for you?

Table 1 lists some of the features of good instructional design, or those things that make learning easy.

Take another look at the things that made learning easy for you. How many are covered in Table 1?

Here's looking at best practice

The one thing that can be said about instructional design is that it's not rocket science. In fact, it should embody what all of us think and feel about what makes for a good and effective learning experience. However, on some

Table 1

WHAT MAKES FOR GOOD INSTRUCTIONAL DESIGN

▮ The content* is structured and sequenced in a way that makes it easy to learn.

▮ The content is presented in a way conducive to the ways in which most adults prefer to learn.

▮ The content can be seen to relate directly to explicit objectives which, in turn, relate to what is required in the workplace.

▮ The means by which the learning is delivered is an effective way of learning the content.

▮ The learning is delivered in bite-sized, digestible chunks.

▮ Appropriate levels and types of support are available on an individual basis.

▮ Learners have some say in the learning process, whether with regard to the pace, time, place, support or progress of their learning.

▮ Learners are provided with appropriate levels of feedback in relation to their learning.

▮ Learners are allowed at some point to find out what they have learned.

*Content = the subject matter in terms of knowledge and skills.

occasions this is not the case, because those who have designed the training appear to have forgotten the basic principles of their art and have gone off on various flights of fancy that only they can justify – sometimes with considerable difficulty.

So what is it that instructional designers need to bear in mind when designing training? Is there a process to ensure that learning occupies the central ground, a process where all the other aspects are used to support it? In short, are there any best-practice guidelines for people to use?

A systematic approach

For many years there has been one approach used by the designers of training to outstanding effect. In fact, it has been so effective that when one or more elements of this approach are missing, all too often the final result is training provision that fails to hit the mark. Although various names have been given to this approach, its main feature is that it is systematic in both content and process. A systematic approach is, therefore, inherently logical, hierarchical and scientific. Essentially, it is a framework or a formula that imposes an appropriate level of discipline on the providers of training but does not stifle creativity or innovation. So why does it work so well?

Organisations that adopt a systematic approach to their training design usually find that:

∎ training plays an important role in helping to meet organisational objectives

∎ they have been able to define levels of workplace performance for different job roles

∎ they can identify in a valid and reliable manner the existence of real training needs

∎ they are able to design, develop and deliver focused training which is targeted to meet organisational needs

∎ they can assess what any individual member of staff can do as a result of their training

∎ they can prove whether or not the training has been effective

∎ a standardised approach to training design is developed with which everyone can identify

∎ a structured process is adopted which is used consistently to meet all training needs.

What's involved?

Although a systematic approach can be said to reflect nothing but good, common sense and appear to be extremely straightforward and easy to use, in my experience the success of any training programme depends to a considerable extent on the degree to which the framework is used in an appropriate way, as well as on the rigour which is applied to each of its component parts. A formula provides only the rules; it is how these rules are used, and the quality of the facts or data applied to these rules, that will determine the successful use of that formula.

Table 2 shows what I consider to be the main component parts of a systematic approach to training provision.

Table 2

COMPONENT PARTS OF A SYSTEMATIC APPROACH

1 Defining the objectives of the organisation (this should be the starting-point for all training programmes).

2 Establishing performance competences (what staff need to be able to do in the workplace).

3 Conducting a training needs analysis (what the training needs are: of staff in relation to the organisation; of a group of job holders; and of individuals in relation to the objectives of the organisation).

4 Defining the training objectives (what it is that staff will have to be able to do at the end of a training programme) in order to achieve the desired performance competences and to fill any knowledge and skill gaps.

5 Identifying the body of content (the knowledge and skills staff need to acquire).

6 Devising an instructional strategy (how, when and where staff can acquire the knowledge and skills they require – this will result in the selection of appropriate delivery media for the training).

7 Designing and developing the training programme in accordance with the instructional strategy (designing and developing all the training materials, and skilling the human resources required for delivering the training event).

8 Developing the assessment tools for the training programme (how staff will be assessed on their achievement of the objectives).

9 Validating and piloting the training programme and the assessment tools (making sure that the training is technically valid and that the training and the assessment tools are valid and reliable when they are used by the staff for whom they are both intended).

10 Revising the training programme and the assessment tools as appropriate (as a result of 9).

11 Delivering the training programme (the training goes 'live').

12 Evaluating the effectiveness of the training programme (determining how effective the training has been in terms of learning and the transfer of that learning into workplace performance).

13 Maintaining the training programme (updating the training material as and when necessary).

14 Redesigning or terminating the training programme (when the training is no longer effective; or where the competences of job holders have changed, which will dictate a need to redesign the training programme; or when the training has satisfied the organisation's objectives).

In brief

- Good instructional design is probably the most important feature of effective training.

- Instructional design is about the way in which the training is structured and sequenced in relation to people's learning needs.

- Instructional design has to take into account the means by which the training is going to be delivered, so that it uses the latter to the full.

- Instructional design is a not a nice, clear entity which owns a distinct set of rules. However, there are best-practice guidelines that can be used.

- Instructional design is concerned with the processes by which adults learn.

- Good instructional design allows all of us to experience the 'eureka' factor and to learn with the minimum of stress and tribulation.

- In order to get the very best out of good instructional design, in terms of cost-effective learning, all training provision should be based on a systematic approach.

2

Getting to Grips with Technology-Based Training

Introduction

'You got a problem with them people learning, luv? If you ask me, they just need a good old dose of TBT – that'll put 'em right.' Apart from sounding like a new mutant disease, TBT (or, to give its full title, technology-based training) has become something of a buzz word over recent years – and for good reasons. However, it is not the panacea for all training ills, in spite of what others might claim!

Using technology in training is not exactly new. In fact, the use of technology applied to learning goes back as far as the 1920s, when Samuel L. Pressey invented a teaching machine to mark multiple-choice questions. In the 1960s teaching machines and programmed learning came to the fore, and during the 1970s devices like tape-slide, tape-filmstrip and mainframe systems were used as a means of providing people with different forms of learning. The 1980s saw the advent of the desktop or microcomputer; technological developments meant that colour became possible, along with the use of graphics and animation. Another feature of this period was interactive video, where a laser disk player was connected to a microcomputer in order to display moving pictures at the same time as other types of content.

Today we have multimedia computers with huge amounts of memory and incredibly fast operating speeds that are capable of handling text, graphics, animation, audio and video, plus the ability to distribute training programmes on CD-ROMs or over the Internet. Use of the Internet and company intranets and extranets have also given rise to such terms as 'online learning', 'web-based training' and 'e-learning', all of which can be regarded as various forms of technology-based learning. (More is said about these below.) In addition, we shouldn't forget the other forms of technology that are also used in training, such as overhead projectors, video and audio cassettes, and even paper-based training – well, after all, technology is used to produce the final product!

So what is TBT?

Broadly speaking, the term TBT can be applied to any situation where technology is used in order to provide training or where it is the means by which the training is made available to the end user. In this sense most people would agree that TBT has been with us a long time, although as the technology has become more and more sophisticated, so have the means by which it has been used in training. Today TBT is still something of a 'catch-all' term even when it is restricted to the use of just a multimedia computer. Indeed, because most people regard TBT as being about computers and nothing else, I have decided that this is the way in which the term will be used throughout the rest of this book.

However, even when the use of the term TBT is restricted just to computers it can still mean different things to different people. Some people call TBT 'computer-based training' or CBT, whereas others refer to 'e-learning', 'web-based training' (WBT) or 'online' learning. Although all these terms have many things in common, the last three in particular require end users to be connected electronically via a network of some description or another. Networks can be local, such as those in a department or a small organisation, or wide – where many departments and users can communicate with one another, and access and share files or applications. In addition, users can be connected via the Internet or through an intranet (which is specific to a group of users, usually within an organisation) or an extranet (which is also an intranet, but one that allows access to other, selected, external users as well).

As far as this book is concerned, I am going to use the term TBT to refer to training that involves the use of a multimedia computer, which can be either a desktop or laptop, and that is delivered to the user on a CD-ROM, over a local area network (LAN), a wide area network (WAN), or via the Internet, an intranet or extranet.

Using TBT

Essentially, TBT is commonly used in one of two main ways:

∎ It can be used for training in relation to technology, ie information technology (IT) and computer systems, hardware, software, process, and procedures.

∎ It can be used for training in relation to non-IT or computer uses.

TBT can in either case be generic (general purpose) or bespoke (designed for a specific purpose or organisation).

TBT for IT

For many years TBT has been used in order to train people in various aspects of IT – well, it does make sense, doesn't it? There are a whole range of applications that fit into this category – for example, *generic* training programmes to show people how to use various computer applications sold on the open market, and *bespoke* programmes to show people how to use new computer systems and organisation-specific software.

This type of TBT can be presented in different ways. It can be:

- a copy of the actual system or software, accompanied by some form of separate instruction (eg instructor-led or tutor-supported, or via a workbook or other form of paper-based training)
- a copy of the actual system or software with the instruction embedded into it
- a simulation of the system or software which is built around the instruction.

TBT for everything else?

Over the years people have also used TBT to produce learning programmes across a whole range of subject areas, all of which have nothing whatsoever to do with IT or computers. Some of this TBT has been produced for general, off-the-shelf purchase, because it covers generic knowledge and skills, such as various aspects of management development, interpersonal skills, financial management, health and safety and so on. Other programmes, meanwhile, have been produced for a specific organisation to use in order to provide bespoke training for particular groups of people.

It used to be thought that using TBT for anything other than IT was restricted only to conveying knowledge. Although this may have been largely true in the days when text was the only viable means of presenting the learning content, nowadays it is generally accepted that TBT can be used not only to acquire knowledge but also to acquire and develop a whole range of skills, in particular cognitive or thinking skills such as problem-solving, as well as other forms of analysis, synthesis, and evaluation or judgements, in addition to psychomotor or manipulative skills. However, the one thing that TBT cannot do as yet is deal wholly with behavioural or affective skills: other forms of training are required for these needs, such as face-to-face learning or action learning.

My, what big teeth you have!

In so many ways the increasing use of TBT is related directly to improvements in computer technology over the last 30 years. Each technological step along the way has seen a similar increase in the use of TBT, as people have realised just what can be achieved at any given point – things that had simply not been possible before. However, the main problem is that with each step along the way the demands on instructional design have also increased and, with them, the greater damage that can be wrought when instructional design is inadequate. So what exactly is possible right now? And what about the not-too-distant future as well? What challenges are posed for instructional designers everywhere?

Text

This can be likened to the 'grandmother' of TBT, because it appears to have been with us since time immemorial. Instead of pages and pages of similar-sized monochrome words, text can now be presented in a variety of styles (fonts), sizes and colours. Text can also appear anywhere and at any time, in the form of boxes, instructions, feedback, as an explanation and as a summary of the main learning points.

Graphics

Although not so old as text, graphics are somewhat like the wolf dressed up in grandmother's clothes. The use of graphics, rather crude in the early days, are now *de rigeur* in any modern TBT programme. Graphics have a major role to play in the overall look and feel of all TBT programmes, ie the user interface, as well as to illustrate learning-points and to simulate software and systems screens. Many different types of graphic can be used, from diagrams, drawings, screen prints and cartoons to icons and buttons, still images and 3-D effects, all of which can be in glorious colour and an amazing degree of resolution or clarity. Just imagine opening a really high-quality glossy book superbly laid out with stunning colours and pictures, and that's exactly what can be done today with TBT. However, graphics should be there to enhance and facilitate the learning, not overwhelm it!

Animation

Taking graphics and making them 'move' is what animation is all about. From simple and often clumsy beginnings there are now some excellent examples of high-quality animations incorporated into many TBT programmes, which are almost comparable to watching a cartoon-type film. A fairly recent development of this art can be seen in the use of virtual reality. This is where graphics are animated to such a high standard of design and resolution that it would appear for all the world that you are actually there! For example, you can now walk around rooms, move things about and interact with objects. If you have ever played some computer games recently you will know exactly what I mean. Reality – what's reality?

Audio

This has probably been the largest breakthrough in TBT. Whereas before words were everything (indeed they were the only thing), we can now replace so much of that text with audio. If you think for a moment about watching something on TV, just how much do you take on board through what you see (moving pictures), what you read (headlines, captions, quotes) and what you hear?

Most of us are extremely competent aurally because, for those of us who do not have hearing disabilities, what we hear is how we interpret much of our world. We may read less but we probably hear much, much more. Although pictures are extremely important, just try watching something on TV with the sound switched off – for example, sport. Unless the commentators are dire, most of us would prefer to hear what they are saying simply because they are probably explaining what is happening, giving us their opinion of events (yes, I admit, this can sometimes be of dubious value or greatly irritating) and, perhaps most importantly, providing the aural cement that binds together the visual images being broadcast. However, just like TV, the use of audio in TBT usually needs to be of the highest order both in terms of voice and broadcast quality.

Video

Probably the second most important advance in recent years has been the ability to incorporate moving pictures of video quality into TBT programmes. It is now possible to show (from quarter-screen to full-screen) high-quality video footage which can range from 'talking heads' to specifically enacted scenarios in order to introduce, demonstrate or reinforce learning-points. As with a TV-type video, it is also possible to pause, replay and fast forward TBT video in relation to any specific learning-point. So, along with graphics and animation, we now have another valuable and powerful means of visual stimulus and input at our disposal.

Interaction

'And now, ladies and gentleman, please let me hear your appreciation for Miss Red Riding Hood!' Too right, for here is our often underrated TBT star who, although she can be much misunderstood and abused, can save the day at the last moment. From an instructional design point of view, interaction is perhaps one of the most powerful of all TBT facilities – indeed, it really makes TBT what it is.

Interaction can take many forms; it should certainly not be restricted to just clicking on 'Next' or hitting the spacebar in order to move forward. There are different types of interaction, which can be placed under these headings:

- control
- involvement
- feedback
- variety.

Here are just some of the things that can be achieved under each of these headings:

- Control:
  - learning at your own pace
  - deciding what parts of the programme you wish to repeat
  - pausing, starting and stopping the audio or video when you want
  - deciding at what point you want to move on to the next frame
  - repeating or advancing a few frames at any time
  - 'bookmarking' a frame to return to at a later stage
  - choosing which objects on the screen you want to look at in order to find out more
  - being able to exit the programme at any stage
  - being able to return to the programme from the point at which you left off.
- Involvement:
  - deciding what part of the TBT programme you want to study, and when
  - deciding the order in which you are going to study the various parts of the programme
  - clicking on diagrams and other objects, or moving them or parts of them around
  - receiving one-to-one instruction from your electronic tutor.
- Feedback:
  - being able to use on-screen help at any stage
  - being asked questions and answering them via

keyboard input or by selecting an answer or answers

☐ being provided with feedback after each learning point has been covered

☐ doing pre-tests or self-assessment quizzes to see how much you already know or can do

☐ doing post-tests or mastery tests to find out how much you have learned and whether you need to study any parts of the programme again.

∎ Variety:

☐ responding to different forms of input such as text, audio, video and graphical information

☐ using other learning materials or aids, or information such as workbooks, worksheets, handouts, data tables, calculations etc.

Although not all TBT programmes contain all of the above types of interaction, the list serves to show just what types of interaction are possible.

TBT in action

Here are the main ways in which TBT is commonly used, along with a description of their most important features.

Distance learning

Although not all TBT is in the form of distance learning, a lot of it is. This is because TBT is an excellent way of delivering training to a widely dispersed audience. However, as with all types of distance learning, it is dangerous to make the assumption that any TBT programme can stand on its own. Depending on the subject matter or content covered, there may be the need to provide some additional learning support for part or all of the target audience. This support can take a variety of forms, such as help desks, coaching, tutoring, discussion groups or action learning back in the workplace.

Some organisations have specially equipped learning centres for staff to use when undertaking any form of distance learning. These centres not only provide a conducive environment in which to learn but also (usually) have an administrator or supervisor present who can in certain situations offer additional learning support or who has access to a subject-matter help desk. One of the advantages of this set-up is that help with using the technology is always on hand because, although TBT programmes should always be designed to be user-friendly, it's a fact of life that computers may be user-hostile!

The increasing trend, though, is away from learning centres and towards delivering TBT online via an organisation's intranet or the Internet. There are two main reasons for this:

▮ TBT can be delivered at a distance to any location, whether at a person's desk, to their home, in a hotel, in a learning centre or to somewhere else in the workplace, thus making it available to all who want it irrespective of where they happen to be at the time they wish to learn.

▮ Delivering TBT online means that only one copy of the programme is required, which makes it far less costly in the long run. Hundreds and thousands of CD-ROMs do not need to be produced and distributed to end users and, when the programme needs to be updated or changed in any way, it only has to be done to the one programme, making the whole process much cheaper and efficient in comparison with CD-ROM delivery.

Online delivery and e-learning provide additional opportunities for the instructional designer: the integration and use of human support at a distance. This support can be either asynchronous (not at the same time) or synchronous (at the same time or 'live'). For example, users can be provided with 'chat rooms' and other forms of peer group support, such as discussion groups, via computer conferencing facilities, newsgroups and bulletin boards. There can also be a tutor available at the other end of the telephone line or accessible via e-mail. Where bandwidth (the amount of data that can be carried along telephone lines or networks at the same time) permits, synchronous communication can take place at the same time as using the TBT programme. Video-cams allow the tutor to see the user and vice versa; this may or may not be a good thing, depending on circumstances – after all, because the online delivery of TBT programmes means any time, any place, you might not want to be seen studying in your 'jim-jams'!

One-to-one learning

One of the most important features of TBT is that the user can be treated on an individual basis. It has long been said that the most effective form of learning is that conducted one on one. You may be familiar with the saying 'sitting by Nellie', where the trainee receives their instruction from 'Nellie', listening, watching and copying her (or him!); this was once the main way of training new staff. However, in our cost-conscious age – and much to the chagrin of some people – the 'Nellie technique' has fallen into disrepute, mainly because it is so time- and resource-consuming, and hence expensive, as well as notoriously prone to the transmission of inconsistent messages and practices. Instead, people are often now herded into classrooms to receive their training, irrespective of whether this form of delivery is the most appropriate.

To a large extent, the computer has restored this balance, because a well-designed TBT programme, irrespective of whether it is delivered on a stand-alone or networked machine, is capable of providing one-to-one learning. It really can be like having your own personal instructor or tutor – just one that happens to be in the form of a TBT programme. And when this is combined with other types of support, it can be argued that one-to-one learning, which is almost akin to being with dear old Nellie, is surely back big-time.

Group learning

Another useful feature of TBT is that it can be used not just on a one-to-one basis but also, depending on the subject matter or content, by several people who are learning together in a group. Although this is not a common use of TBT it is, nonetheless, a very powerful one, particularly where the need to discuss key learning or action points is concerned.

Self-managed learning

TBT also offers people the opportunity to manage their own learning. Unless otherwise required, such as when a new system is being introduced and people are instructed to undertake their learning at a specific time and in a specific way, TBT programmes can be designed so that users can take control of their own learning and manage it in a way conducive to them. This can also bring with it a number of problems, most notably people's ability – or lack of it – to manage their own learning. Because a lot of us have been used to being told what to learn, when to learn and even how to learn, self-managed learning can prove to be something of a daunting challenge to even the most experienced participant.

Student and performance management

Just as a computer can act as a personal tutor, so it can track and monitor who does what, when and where. Learning management systems have grown in importance over the years. From relatively humble beginnings, when specific information was stored on a floppy disk, to today's extremely sophisticated systems that can capture and transfer all manner of information to a central source for later analysis, these systems are now regarded, particularly in large organisations, as an indispensable part of most

TBT provision, particularly for that delivered online.

Here are some of the things that can be captured by these systems:

- personal details of users (eg name, staff number, area, department, region)
- training details (eg day and date undertaken, time taken – both total and elapsed, parts of the course studied)
- assessment details (eg type of help required, feedback provided, pre-test and post-test scores, re-study requirements)
- evaluation details (eg reactions to the training)
- other personal details (eg appraisal reviews, personal development plans, training and development received or yet to be undertaken)
- other training details (eg courses available, course requirements, rooms or space available, bookings made, joining instructions, briefing and de-briefing requirements, trainers available).

Performance support

Electronic performance support systems (EPSSs) have also been around for some time but, with the advent of online learning and e-learning, they have now come into their own. Essentially, they are a means of providing online assistance in the form of help or 'wizards' when learning, for example, to use a software program or a business process. An EPSS can be built into the actual programme, just as the 'Help' facility is in many software products, which allows it to be used in a stand-alone capacity, or it can exist separately, as well as being accessed over a network. EPSS and student/performance management systems are also provided, along with a whole range of training courses to form complete e-learning or online infrastructures, sometimes called 'web-enabled learning systems', designed to be accessed via an organisation's intranet or over the Internet via a 'learning portal'.

But is TBT always the answer?

Now this is where the action really starts. Having looked at what TBT is all about and how it can be used, the really big question is under what circumstances it should be used. Put simply, when should you think, 'Yes, it's got to be TBT' or 'No, I don't think so'?

Although TBT has a lot to offer, it should never be regarded as the total solution to meet all learning needs. There are many situations where it is clearly unsuitable, such as when dealing with the development of interpersonal skills and behaviours, and others where it might form part of the overall solution, for example when it is combined with different types of distance learning, face-to-face learning or action learning. So, what are the things you need to consider when deciding whether TBT should constitute a part of any particular learning provision or whether it should be the total solution?

Learning needs and learning objectives

The first thing to consider when deciding whether TBT is an appropriate solution or not is the nature of the learning needs or objectives in question. Because training should never be provided in the absence of any identified learning needs, this information must be readily to hand. So what is it exactly that people need to learn: is it knowledge, is it skills – and, if so, what kind of skills – or is it a change of behaviour?

Where a large amount of knowledge is required, particularly if this can be presented in an interactive way, then TBT can most certainly be considered an option. Likewise, if cognitive skills are required, such as applying, analysing, and synthesising knowledge, then TBT can also be considered, as it can if psychomotor or manipulative skills are involved, such as simulating the use of equipment along with various processes and procedures. When it comes to other types of skill, like interpersonal ones, TBT can still be considered if, for example, some underlying knowledge is required, or if different examples of applying these skills need to be included.

Learning gaps

Because TBT, particularly bespoke TBT, is not cheap to produce, it is important to know the extent of any learning gaps. This means knowing, in relation to the learning needs identified previously, approximately how much learning is required to satisfy each of the learning objectives. If the learning gaps are fairly small for everyone, then using TBT, unless it is a fairly inexpensive generic programme, may be rather like using a sledgehammer to crack a nut! However, if the majority of people in question have large learning gaps, then TBT might be a cost-effective solution.

Content or subject matter

I know it's blindingly obvious to say so, but where the content or subject matter of the learning needs or objectives have anything to do with computers, TBT provision has to be a very serious contender. After all, if people have to learn how to use new computer software or systems, or processes and procedures based upon them, then what better from an instructional point of view than letting them use the actual technology? Just think what it would be like trying to learn how to use some new computer software by just reading a manual – thanks, but no thanks!

Where the content is not computer-related but is quite technical or specific in nature, and particularly when its mastery requires application, practice and feedback, then TBT should be considered. TBT should also be considered if it is important to ensure that consistent messages are conveyed to all those involved, and where other forms of delivery might allow for inconsistency to creep in, such as with face-to-face learning, which can involve a number of trainers.

Volatility of content

The other important aspect in relation to content is its volatility. A major consideration must be just how stable the content is going to be. For example, if a computer system is still in the process of development or additional versions are in the pipeline in the very near future, then the costs of producing a total TBT solution may not be worth it. Likewise, if there is a lot of content that is likely to change again and again, the use of TBT, along with how such content is dealt with, needs to be considered most carefully. With modern authoring software it is possible to create libraries of 'volatile' material so that when changes are required they have only to be effected in one place. Even so – and this also applies to delivering TBT online – if a lot of content is likely to change on a frequent basis (for example, interest rates), due care must be exercised. Mind you, because reprinting paper-based materials can work out to be even more expensive, the decision is not that clear-cut, but it is an important issue to bear in mind nevertheless.

Target audience

Someone once said, 'Don't ever provide training when you don't know who it is for.' I'm not sure how generic training providers get around this one, unless they have done a lot of market research, but nonetheless it's an important point to make. In relation to TBT there are three vital things to know about the target audience whose learning needs have already been identified:

∎ the size – how many people are involved
∎ the location – where they are based
∎ the profile – are they a heterogeneous (mixed) group or a homogeneous one?

The larger the number of people, the more economical distance learning – and, therefore, TBT – will be. Conversely, of course, when a small number of people is involved, the more expensive TBT provision will be per person. The more geographically dispersed the target audience, then (again) the more cost-effective distance learning and TBT provision are likely to be.

Finally, what is known about the target audience in terms of who they are, where they come from, what their previous experience is, plus their ages, job roles, gender and (if any) disabilities (eg visual or aural impairment), and so on? This information is vital, because it will determine whether the target audience constitutes a homogeneous (single) group or whether it needs to be segmented in some way. It can also mean that the target audience has to be segmented in relation to their learning needs, such as when a new computer system is introduced for two or more different job roles and where each role involves mastering slightly different learning objectives. Although the latter may or may not affect the decision to use TBT in the first instance, it will certainly have a major effect on how the training is designed once it has been decided to use TBT. (It may very well affect the decision to use TBT, though, if there are many different segments involved, thereby reducing the overall numbers involved and increasing the complexity of the final solution.)

Time available

As one of the advantages of well-designed TBT is that it can be undertaken anywhere and at any time, if the time available for training (particularly in one go) is limited, then being able to use it on an as-and-when basis may be just the answer. One of the reasons given by a number of large corporate organisations for their use of online learning or e-learning is that it doesn't take up so much time, because staff are not away from the workplace for as long as they would be if they attended a course. Whether the learning received online is as effective as other forms of learning is, of course, another matter, but nevertheless the time argument is a hard one to refute.

Learning environments

Another factor to consider is the different environments available for learning. For example, if TBT is a possibility, then where can it be undertaken – in a learning centre, in the workplace, at people's desks or at home? Whichever options are available, it is essential that they are conducive to learning and to mastering the learning objectives of the programme in question. For example, using a TBT programme at your desk in the workplace may be acceptable if you can be guaranteed peace and quiet with no interruptions, or if it is needed for performance support, such as to refresh your knowledge on some key points. The use of TBT will also need to fit into the organisation's culture and overall training policy, particularly when people are expected to undertake their training outside normal working hours or in locations not managed or provided by the organisation.

Availability of equipment

It goes without saying that one of the most important factors when considering the use of TBT is whether sufficient equipment is available. Although more and more people now use computers as part of their daily work, not everyone does or probably ever will. Even when TBT is to be used away from a person's desk, it is still necessary to think 'equipment' unless, of course, the target audience all have laptops. However, it may not always be enough for everyone to have access to a computer, because it's also vital that the technical specification of the machine is capable of running either a generic TBT programme or can cope with the demands of a bespoke one. If the TBT is to be accessed online, computers will need to be networked in some way or people provided with Internet access.

Training budget and time available

The other factor to be considered when deciding whether TBT is viable or not is the amount of budget available and the time available, particularly if a bespoke training solution is required. Even buying generic TBT programmes may not work out to be as cheap as first appears, particularly if site licences (where many users are involved) and support or maintenance contracts have to be entered into.

Bespoke TBT is never a cheap option, although it can work out to be very economical in the long run. The cost of producing one hour's worth of multimedia TBT will be in the tens of thousands of pounds bracket, making the up-front costs high particularly when compared with face-to-face learning or some other forms of distance learning. However, once the programme is up and running the on-going costs are relatively small, particularly when compared with face-to-face learning; and if the programme has a long 'shelf-life', during which it will be used by a large number of people, the up-front costs can be justified more easily. The other thing to bear in mind is the time available for producing bespoke TBT. Compared with all other forms of training, the development ratios required to produce one hour of TBT are several times greater. Although you may be able to design a short face-to-face course in a week or so, it will take at least a month to produce even a small bespoke TBT programme.

Thinking TBT?

The most important thing to remember is that none of the above is mutually exclusive. You will very rarely, if ever, be able to 'think TBT' if only one of the categories for consideration shouts yes at you! Only if there are several instances where you think 'TBT' should you then consider carefully its possible use. Having said that, it is more likely than not, especially given the wide-ranging and appropriate uses of TBT, that you could very well end up thinking, 'Ah, TBT!'

> If you have ever used any TBT, think back to the last programme that you used and then ask yourself:
>
> ■ Was it appropriate for my learning needs/ objectives?
>
> ■ Was it appropriate in relation to the subject matter or content that it covered?
>
> ■ Was it suitable for the amount of time I had for learning and in relation to where I used it?

In brief

■ Technology-based training (TBT) has its strengths and its weaknesses – meaning that it is not always the most appropriate solution for some training needs.

■ Technology has been used in training for a long time, but with each technological step along the way a commensurate rise in its use in learning has also come.

■ TBT is a term that can be used in a number of different ways – it can encompass CBT, WBT, online learning and e-learning.

■ TBT can be used on stand-alone or networked multimedia computers (via LANs, WANs, intranets, extranets or the Internet).

■ TBT can be used for IT-type training or non-computer-related learning, and it can also be generic or bespoke in nature.

■ TBT is very useful for acquiring and developing knowledge, cognitive and psychomotor skills. What it cannot do wholly as yet – and possibly never will – is to develop behaviours or affective skills.

■ TBT can use a combination of text, graphics, animation, audio and video, and support the use of these through a variety of different forms of interaction.

■ TBT can be used as a form of distance learning, one-to-one learning, group learning and self-managed learning. It can also be used in conjunction with learning (student and performance) management systems and electronic performance support systems.

▮ When deciding whether to use TBT, it is of utmost importance to consider:

☐ the learning needs and learning objectives

☐ the learning gaps

☐ the content or subject matter

☐ the volatility of the content

☐ the target audience

☐ the time available for learning

☐ the places where learning can take place

☐ the equipment available

☐ the training budget and the amount of development time available.

▮ Deciding to use TBT is not a one-dimensional decision – there are many factors to be considered.

3

The Bare Necessities

Introduction

When it comes to instructional design, TBT is probably the most demanding medium of all: get it wrong and it will stay wrong until the programme is rewritten. At least with classroom-based training you can modify your approach or materials as you go along if things are not quite right. Although all forms of distance learning suffer from this lack of modification, TBT suffers the most because it is now used extensively, is expensive and time-consuming to produce, and so much is expected of it in terms of what it can achieve in relation to learning.

So when it comes to TBT, not only must the instructional design be of the highest order but also, because of TBT's incredible power and potential, the demands placed on the instructional designer are the greatest they are ever likely to be. Although the basic principles of instructional design are the same irrespective of the medium used, the actual knowledge and skills required for TBT are more extensive and detailed. This, coupled with the need for very few or no errors, means that highly specialised skills and extensive experience are absolutely essential. However, this should not put the beginner or less experienced person off, because we all have to start somewhere; it does mean, though, that the necessary skills cannot be acquired overnight, and that for most ordinary mortals they will take a number of years to be developed fully.

In this chapter I'm going to look at the essentials of instructional design as far as TBT is concerned. The emphasis is on the word 'essential', because if one or more of these are missing then the overall instructional design is going to be compromised. Then, in the following chapters, I shall look at some of these essentials in more detail. Although what follows is aimed specifically at the production of bespoke TBT, much of it can and should be applied to generic TBT programmes as well.

As you work through this chapter try asking yourself the following:

∎ Is this something I do on a regular basis?
∎ Is this something which I would expect others to do on my behalf?
∎ Why is this essential, and do I understand what is likely to happen if it is omitted for any reason?

This is what I need!

The starting-point for any instructional design and all TBT provision is a needs analysis of some description. Some people refer to these as training needs analyses (TNAs), which is fine, provided they are not just looking for training needs at the expense of other learning needs. The reasons for conducting a needs analysis can be many and varied, such as where:

∎ the organisation is not meeting its objectives or targets
∎ specific groups of job holders are not performing to the standards required
∎ individuals are performing below par
∎ an existing course is proving no longer to be effective.

In identifying learning needs, consideration has to be given not only to what learning needs actually exist, and to what extent they can be met through training, but also to nonlearning-related needs that may have a negative effect on any subsequent provision. I am not alone in asking how you can possibly provide any form of training when you haven't established first whether there is any need for it, let alone precisely what those needs are. To my mind there is only one answer to anyone who ever says that identifying learning needs is not necessary or a waste of time: 'You can*not* be serious!'

Establishing learning needs

Exactly how do you establish learning needs? Well, if you are looking for learning needs related to workplace performance, you need to find out what it is that people are supposed to be doing in the workplace in relation to the knowledge and skills (competences) and behaviours (competencies) they require. Having defined the desired performance competencies, you can then measure to what extent people possess them, ie their actual performance competencies, and so identify their performance needs. From here it is then a matter of deciding which of these needs can be translated into learning needs and, in the context of this book, particularly those that can be met by some form of training, as opposed to those that may be related to other matters such as poor motivation or environmental factors.

Having established any learning needs that can be addressed by some form of training provision, it is then a matter of translating these competences (knowledge and skills) into learning objectives. Note here the deliberate omission of competencies (behaviours), purely because training is not the most suitable vehicle for developing these, although other development activities most certainly are.

Learning objectives

Learning objectives are descriptions of what people are expected to be able to do during and at the end of a training programme or some other form of development activity.

In this way they differ from competencies in terms of both their purpose and wording or construction. For example, although a competency may be along the lines of 'To provide a high level of customer care at all times', a learning objective in relation to this desired level of workplace performance might read 'To explain the benefits to the organisation of providing appropriate feedback to a customer when handling a complaint.' Although there are some who say that learning objectives are not only time-consuming to produce but also sound like the utterings of a demonic robot – 'At the end of your instruction you will be able to pick out six items which…' – without them it's virtually impossible to get the instructional design right.

Table 3 on page 34 shows some important things to consider when thinking about learning objectives.

To write attainable, observable and measurable objectives is not something that most people can do in an odd few minutes: they take time, skill and patience to get right. However, once you have got them right, here is what you can do with them:

You can use them to identify the content or subject matter for the training programme.

■ They can be built into the training programme so that participants know what is expected of them at various stages; it's fine to rewrite them for this purpose, provided they do not lose their meaning or become ambiguous.

■ They will provide you with some sound criteria if you are looking for a generic training programme, although finding the same in some off-the-shelf programmes may not be so straightforward!

■ They will help you to make sure that only essential content is covered and that the training programme is focused totally on what it is that people need to learn.

■ By defining them as terminal and enabling objectives you can use them to help structure and sequence the

Table 3

LEARNING OBJECTIVES

- Competencies are definitions of workplace performance, whereas learning objectives are definitions of what people are supposed to be able to do at the end of a period of learning.
- To assume that competencies and objectives are one and the same is unhelpful because:
  - it may not be possible to cover all the competencies in the learning objectives: there may be some aspects of performance that are not going to be improved by learning
  - some of the competencies may be addressed best by training and some by other forms of learning
  - training objectives are usually concerned with knowledge and skills and not behaviours, whereas other learning objectives may address behaviours as well.
- Learning objectives should be attainable, observable and measurable.
- Learning objectives should be attainable because training is not a norm-referenced activity, ie it is not designed to ensure that some people fail.
- Learning objectives should be observable because it is important for people to be able to show in some explicit way that they have mastered them.
- Learning objectives should be measurable because, if they aren't, how will anyone know whether they have been mastered?
- Learning objectives should always contain an 'action verb' which describes what the person is supposed to be able to do, eg 'state', 'list', 'describe', 'explain', 'demonstrate', and this must be an *observable* action.
- Learning objectives should always contain a description of the knowledge or skills that the person is required to demonstrate and they must be ones that, along with the 'action verb', are capable of being measured.
- Learning objectives can also contain a statement of performance that will be measured, as well as the conditions in which the objective will be observed.
- Learning objectives can also be classified as enabling (those that describe small learning steps) and *terminal* (those that require a number of enabling objectives to have been mastered first).

learning in the most effective way to ensure their mastery.

- When it comes to testing or assessing participants on their mastery of the objectives, the enabling objectives can be used as criteria for feedback and the terminal objectives for mastery or end tests.

Now perhaps you can see why I, for one, cannot understand those who say that you don't need objectives for producing or selecting a training programme, or any other type of learning activity come to that. If I do not know what it is that people are expected to be able to do at the end of a training programme, if I do not have at my disposal these essential building blocks, then I would struggle greatly to design or select any form of training that was effective both in terms of learning and in relation to workplace performance.

Who is the training for?

Another – but often overlooked – essential is profiling the target audience. Because training and particularly TBT are designed to meet the needs of a large number of people, it is essential to know something about the target audience before getting down to producing or selecting a programme with the potential to meet their needs. The easiest way of profiling your target audience is to do it when the TNA or needs analysis is being carried out. This is because you will probably be in some form of contact with the target audience at this stage, so it makes an ideal opportunity to find out more about them. If this isn't possible (for example, when analysing an existing course where perhaps limited contact with the target audience is required), you should still build target audience profiling as a task into your overall project plan.

Table 4 on page 36 lists some of the things that you may need to find out about your target audience.

Segmenting a target audience

People in marketing have been doing this for a long time. They have realised that if you are going to sell a product then you need to know exactly to whom you are going to sell it; treating your target audience as homogeneous when they are not can lead to disaster. When all the relevant

Table 4

TARGET AUDIENCE PROFILING

- ▌ Approximately how large is the target audience – how many people are you dealing with?
- ▌ Do they all do the same job or do they have different job roles?
- ▌ Do they all have the same learning needs in terms of competenc(i)es and/or learning objectives?
- ▌ What else do you know about them that may be relevant in terms of:
  - ☐ age and gender
  - ☐ experience, career paths, qualifications, previous use of TBT, learning difficulties and disabilities
  - ☐ location, working environment, and access to training and associated resources?
- ▌ Do you need to segment the target audience, and, if so, in what ways?

---

information has been collected, it needs then to be analysed to see whether the target audience consists of more than one distinct group or segment.

There is no single specific way to segment a target audience: it all depends on how the characteristics of the audience differ, and whether these differences are important or not. Here are some characteristics on which you might need to segment your audience in certain circumstances:

- ▌ *Size*: the size of the target audience might be so large that, irrespective of any other factors, in order to provide adequate levels of support it is necessary to 'roll out' the training, which means breaking the total group into small-sized segments. This may also be the case when a new computer system, processes and procedures are rolled out across an organisation.
- ▌ *Job role*: although the target audience may have the same learning needs, they may not all perform the same job role. Depending on the training objectives, a conscious decision may be made to customise the training to suit specific job roles, or to ensure that the training is designed for people with different job

holders (eg as may be the case in a team-building programme). Also, in some organisations where rank and seniority are all-important, treating senior executives and junior staff in exactly the same way may not go down very well, especially with the former!

▌ *Learning needs*: people with different learning needs have to be treated differently. It sounds so obvious, but often the small differences in learning needs can be overlooked. Differences in learning needs can result from requiring to do things slightly differently or can arise because, although the nature of the learning may be the same, the width of the gap can vary.

▌ *Age*: although age is becoming far less of a barrier to most things – and that includes learning – there may be some situations where it should be taken into account, for example where the use of technology is encountered for the first time. However, having said that, it is extremely important to avoid stereotyping people because of their age without any supporting evidence: like assuming that all people in their fifties are going to resent the introduction of new technology whereas those in their twenties will snap it up with joyful glee!

▌ *Gender*: as with age, it can be all too easy to jump to false conclusions about the importance of gender differences. However, on the few occasions when gender can make a difference, the audience should be split into male and female groups, such as when dealing with aspects specific to one group that may cause embarrassment to the other.

▌ *Previous experience*: this can take many different forms, probably the most important of which is what people already know and can do in relation to identified learning needs. So often training programmes are designed on the assumption that everyone starts from the same point – zero knowledge and skills – which is very rarely true, unless a brand new system, process or procedure is being introduced. In addition, it is also useful to know where people have come from and what previous jobs they have had, as well as their experience of learning and different forms of training.

- *Career paths*: linked very closely to previous experience is knowing what paths people have trod to arrive at their current job role. Something that may appear, on the face of it, to be new could in fact turn out to be anything but for some of the target audience!

- *Qualifications*: again, there are dangers here of stereotyping by assuming those without any qualifications are 'thick', unmotivated to learn or possessing limited study skills. Knowing what qualifications your target audience possess, however, can give you a feel for whether they can all be treated the same or whether you should take into account differences in levels of conceptual development and the need for learning support.

- *Learning difficulties*: it would be quite wrong to assume that none of us have learning difficulties just because we have reached adulthood. For example, dyslexia is not found only among children: there are adult dyslexics too, and their needs should be recognised when any form of training provision is required. They may just need more time or the opportunity to learn at their own pace, or to be presented with fewer verbal and more aural and visual stimuli.

- *Physical disabilities*: because many organisations are now positive about disability, those with impaired speech, sight or hearing or who have other physical impairments are often carrying out the same jobs as their more able-bodied colleagues. However, this does not mean that when it comes to training they can necessarily be treated the same, because they will have different needs in relation not only to their particular disability but also to how they can learn most effectively.

- *Location*: although location should not be a barrier to accessing training, there are questions of access to consider whether the target audience is widely dispersed or in a central location. Location can also have cultural implications even when the target audience resides in one country and, again, due consideration should be given to this aspect.

- *Working environment*: the conditions in which people work may also influence their ability to learn effectively. For example, are shift workers involved? Are some of the target audience part-time workers? Are working conditions quiet and free from dust and dirt? Does everyone have similar working conditions or are they different? Also, *how* do they work – in teams, on their own, out on the road, with little line management support, or in hierarchical and authoritarian departments or sections?

- *Access to training resources*: does all of the target audience have the same access to training and associated resources? If not, can anything be done about this within available budgets and other constraining factors, or will it need to be taken into account when deciding the form that any training provision should take? This is often a major consideration when thinking about providing any form of TBT, because provision in terms of the basic essentials can vary so widely, as can the extent of IT support. For example, some training departments experience considerable problems when trying to deliver TBT online because of wide variations in IT support, and with the level of co-operation from those involved when it comes to providing the necessary technological infrastructure.

Think information

One of the main problems with target audience profiling is that people often think about it too late in the day. Target audience profiling is as much like carrying out a piece of research as conducting a TNA is. You first need to generate some hypotheses about what is likely to be important and then gather information either to support or refute them. There will not be the time or the need to collect information on all the above, which is where your hunches as a trainer come in. Start by drawing up a list of possible factors that may have an effect on how, where and when you can provide a training solution to meet the learning needs that have been identified. Then work out what information you require, along with how, where and when you can obtain it, and take it from there. Above all, don't fall into the trap of believing that everyone is the same and so can all be treated in exactly the same way!

The all-important blueprint

Another essential is a plan for the instructional design. This is sometimes called an 'instructional strategy', because it describes several aspects fundamental or strategic to the instructional design of the proposed training. An instructional strategy is therefore like a 'blueprint' upon which the training will be built. However, once again, there are some who say preparing one of these is not only time-consuming but in fact a waste of time: after all, why on earth do you need to go away and prepare one of these when you could be far better occupied producing the real thing?

Three little pigs

You probably know the moral of the nursery tale about the three little pigs and their various house-building techniques. When someone says to me that an instructional strategy is not necessary, I use my stock response: 'Would you let someone build you a house without using any architect's plans?' Most sane people would respond with a mighty no: 'What a stupid idea – you could end up with something like the little pig's house built of straw!' Quite. So what is different about 'building' a training programme? Without a plan you are likely to end up with some higgledy-piggledy apology for training, and might even experience the ultimate ignominy of being responsible for providing something that not only fails abjectly but also does considerable harm in the process. So who in their right mind would ever be prepared to take such a risk? (Surely a rhetorical question, methinks!)

Shades of blue

So exactly what does need to go into the blueprint or instructional strategy? Table 5 lists some things that should be considered.

Table 5

INSTRUCTIONAL STRATEGIES

- Overall brief for the training programme.
- Profile of the target audience.
- Key aims and terminal learning objectives.
- Overall structure and sequence of the training.
- Programme map.
- Assessment strategy.
- Evaluation strategy.
- Recommended delivery media.
- Details of elements, modules, sections:
  - title
  - aims
  - objectives (terminal and enabling)
  - content
  - time for average study
  - teaching/learning points
  - assessment methods.
- Additional information required.

It does not matter whether the training is bespoke or generic: anyone who is involved in designing a training programme and who is worth their salt will need to ensure that an instructional strategy is produced before any further work on the programme is undertaken.

> If at this stage you want to find out more about each of the above, they are described in detail in the next chapter.

What's the 'spec', then?

Assuming that the recommended delivery medium either in whole or in part is TBT, then the next essential is some form of specification (or 'spec') for the training. I call this document a 'briefing and specification' document because, to my mind, it ought to contain all the information required to ensure that every member of the project team (ie all those involved in the design, development and production of the TBT) are, as some are wont to say, singing from the same hymn sheet.

The importance of a briefing and specification document as far as TBT is concerned lies in detailing exactly what is required in order to produce the end product. Irrespective of what some may claim, producing a TBT programme is a team effort which brings people with different skills and experience together. If you meet trainers who tell you they are capable of producing a TBT programme from start to finish on their own, be on the alert, because although they may think they can, in practice it is highly unlikely, particularly if they have very little skill in or experience of instructional design.

It is generally recognised, despite the availability of some 'easy-to-use' authoring or programming tools, that producing high-quality, cost-effective TBT programmes requires people with high levels of skill in instructional design, programming, graphics design, and audio and video production. Depending on the size of a TBT programme, the number of people involved in its production can be quite considerable, and it is a well-known fact that the more people there are involved, the greater possibility there is for misunderstandings and mistakes to creep in. If you doubt this, just ask any IT specialist if they would ever consider programming some software in the absence of a detailed spec. (Be warned, though, that if you do, you may receive some rather strange looks!)

Producing the 'hymn sheet'

What goes into a briefing and specification document will, to some extent, depend upon how much has been put into the instructional strategy and what other documentation exists in relation to the TBT programme.

Table 6 on page 44 lists a number of things to be considered for inclusion in such a document. For some people this list may appear somewhat daunting; if you are one of these, then fear not, for I shall be going into greater detail about all these aspects in this and future chapters.

Once again, it should matter not one jot whether the TBT programme is bespoke or generic, because a briefing and specification document is an indispensable element of *all* TBT production.

> Further information about the user interface, scripts and project planning is provided in this chapter, but if you want to know more about producing a briefing and specification document, you will find it in Chapter 5.

Great graphics!

Have you ever started to use a TBT programme only to think, 'Wow, what great graphics – pity about the learning, though'? Although the importance of graphics in TBT is not in dispute, *how* they are used can be called into question. Leaving aside, for the time being, the use of graphics to enhance learning on an on-going basis

Table 6

BRIEFING AND SPECIFICATION DOCUMENTS

▮ Details of the target audience, including any segments.
▮ General approach – standards and guidelines in relation to the use of:
  ▢ text
  ▢ audio
  ▢ graphics
  ▢ animation
  ▢ video
  ▢ interactions.
▮ User interface.
▮ Navigation features – use of function and navigation buttons in relation to the user interface.
▮ Style, pitch and tone – in line with the target audience, standards and guidelines for the style, pitch and tone of the text, graphics, audio and video.
▮ Assessment – standards and guidelines for both formative (feedback) and summative (mastery) assessment, plus the use of any student or performance management systems or electronic performance support systems.
▮ Script format in relation to:
  ▢ programme-ready material layout (PRMs)
  ▢ nomenclature
  ▢ interactions
  ▢ instructions to members of the production team such as graphic designers and programmers.
▮ Editorial guidelines and conventions to support all the above, but particularly in relation to the scripts or PRMs.
▮ Project plan for all production phases – scripting, asset production (graphics, audio and video), programming, testing (alpha and beta) and validation, and distribution.

throughout a TBT programme, I want to take a look here at one of the most important features of TBT – the user interface.

Immediate reactions

When you first start using a TBT programme, initial impressions are, for good or bad, usually formed quite quickly by what the screen layout or the user interface looks like. For example, is it:

- easy on the eye
- encouraging to use
- conducive to your learning
- easy to use and to find your way around?

All these aspects are vital features of instructional design, because any user interface that does not conform to any or all of the above will have a negative impact on learning. Designing a conducive user interface requires the combined skills of both instructional and graphic designers; it should most certainly not be left to the latter alone!

Prototyping

Before the development of a TBT programme starts in earnest, the production of a prototype is generally regarded as an essential step. In this way it is possible to try out various ideas and layouts in order to produce an appropriate user interface for the target audience. Although the actual production of the prototype rests with graphic designers and programmers, the input from instructional designers is absolutely vital.

The basic idea is to provide a few minutes' worth of a mock-up of the actual programme to show what it will look and feel like in terms of the overall design, the use of menus, where text and graphics will appear and how feedback will be provided. If audio is used it also can be included, provided it does not cost too much to produce; the inclusion of video at this stage may however be too expensive, unless some archive footage can be used.

Although it is tempting to show you at this point an example of a 'good' user interface, I have resisted the temptation for a couple of reasons. To be effective, the design of the user interface should be something that supports both the learning needs and profile of the target audience. In this way it can be regarded as a quite specific entity, even though it may contain some generic or familiar features. As a result it is very common for people to react in quite a negative manner when shown a screen from a TBT programme, unless they have been furnished with all the facts and thinking lying behind its design. The other reason, at least as important, is that I have yet to find a user interface that looks good in just black and white! So, given these constraints, I have decided to use instead a diagram (Figure 1, opposite) which shows you where some of the main features of the user interface might appear on the screen.

Table 7 on page 48 shows some of the factors that need to be taken into account when designing the user interface.

> Now take another look at Table 7. How many of the factors mentioned would have either a positive or negative impact on your learning?
>
> When you have made your assessment, what is your view of involving instructional designers in the design of the user interface?

Vive la différence!

Now there are some who think that using exactly the same user interface for all TBT programmes is a good idea. Well, I for one do not think so, and for these two main reasons:

■ Target audiences are all different. For example, from a needs analysis you may discover that you have a group of people who are quite apprehensive about training or about the subject matter in question. If this is the case then you may, with good reason, make a conscious decision to design a user interface that puts them at rest, encourages them and generally tries to make them feel good. Likewise, you may have a target audience that is somewhat complacent and easy-going about something of vital importance to your organisation. In this case you may decide that a user interface that is vibrant, hard-hitting and 'in-your-face' is far more appropriate.

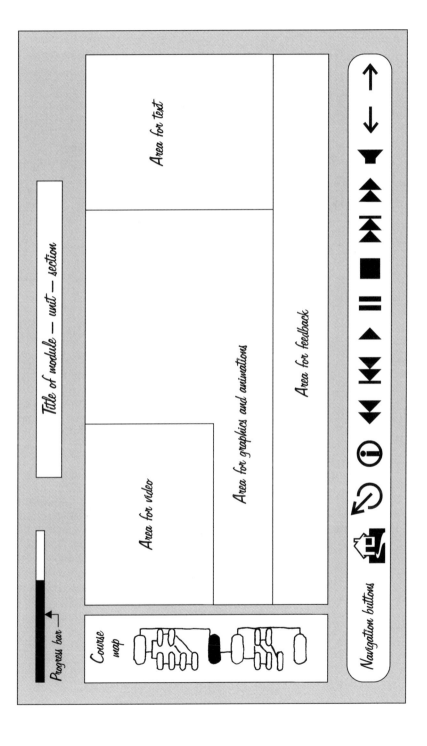

Figure 1

DESIGNING THE USER INTERFACE

Table 7

THE USER INTERFACE

Features	Factors
Easy on the eye	▎ Overall layout/design, eg uncluttered, well laid out, looks good and professional. ▎ Colours, eg well balanced, harmonious. ▎ Font size and type, eg readable, uncluttered, no squinting required!
Encouraging to use	▎ Overall layout/design, eg looks inviting, is not complicated or cluttered, can be understood fairly quickly, IT skills not required! ▎ Colours, eg used to good effect to calm people down, give reassurance or to 'stir them up'. ▎ Graphics, eg fit for their purpose, appropriately displayed, humorous, easy to understand. ▎ Structure, eg clear, accessible, manageable, understandable. ▎ Audio, eg used to good effect, initially either to reassure or to generate interest.
Conducive to learning	▎ Structure, eg logical, explained, easy to manage, well set out. ▎ Navigation buttons, eg obvious with regard to use, comprehensive in terms of functions, available when needed, allow the user to be in control. ▎ Help, eg available at all times, comprehensive in coverage. ▎ Glossary, eg available at all times, easy to use, accurate and helpful descriptions.
Easy to find your way around	▎ Menus, eg accessible at all times, self-explanatory, show what has been completed or what needs to be studied. ▎ Navigation buttons, eg accessible at all times, situated at the bottom of the screen so that left-handed people are not discriminated against, do what they claim to do. ▎ Instructions, eg comprehensive, understandable, accessible at any time. ▎ Help, eg accessible at any time, comprehensive, understandable.

■ Subject matter or content is very different. Ideally the user interface should be designed with the subject matter or content uppermost in mind. What is it that users are supposed to be able to do, how are they supposed to master these objectives, what is their learning all about? Until all these questions are answered it is extremely difficult to decide what will constitute an appropriate design for the user interface. Sure, we can agree on the features that any user interface should have, but how they are used is quite a different matter. Although there may be some occasions when certain overriding factors, for example cost considerations, dictate the use of a common or more generic user interface, it should never just be assumed that one interface will do for all seasons. Where appropriate, using the same navigation buttons to help people find their way around is a good idea, but to provide exactly the same look and feel on each and every occasion is likely to prove extremely misguided and short-sighted. Indeed, I know of a number of organisations that have decided not to use a standard interface, particularly in their bespoke TBT programmes, purely to prevent users from becoming bored with the subject matter – 'Let it be appropriate and different!', users and providers have both been heard to cry!

Scripting it right

Another essential when producing TBT is not, as some people might think, to use some super-duper, easy-peasy authoring software that allows you to develop the programme as you go along – it is by a far lower-tech process, that actually involves using paper as part of the end product!

Producing scripts which usually appear in printed form is essential to all TBT production, because this is where the art of instructional design really comes to the fore. Some people call this stage producing 'programme-ready materials' (PRMs), because these 'state-of-the-arters' would say, quite rightly, that the scripts should contain everything that the programmers have to know to produce the end product.

The most useful scripts describe the graphics, text, audio, video and various interactions as they will actually happen. The whole 'script' or PRM tells the story to all those involved in producing the TBT programme – the graphic designers, the audio and video producers, the programmers, and the people involved in testing the programme before it is released. The problem with the design and layout of some scripts is that that they can be a bit of a 'closed shop' to those who have not had much experience of producing TBT, notably the subject-matter experts and the client or sponsor. By producing the scripts in an easy-to-understand format, everyone involved can get to grips with what they contain and, most importantly, those who need to will be able to sign them off so that the next stages of production can commence.

> If at this stage you want to find out more about scripting TBT, the process is described in detail in Chapter 7.

Perfect planning

The last essential requirement which, if this book was not concentrating on instructional design, would be at the top of the list of priorities is project planning. Producing either a generic or a bespoke TBT programme is like any major project in that high standards of planning and management are required.

If the instructional design and overall development of a TBT programme are to proceed in a timely and conducive manner, it is essential that all the tasks involved in the process are placed in an appropriate order and resourced

Table 8

TBT PROJECT PLANNING AND MANAGEMENT

Factors	Considerations
The production process	▪ What tasks need to be included and in what order? ▪ How much flexibility is required in terms of tasks included and the order in which they are undertaken? ▪ How many tasks can be undertaken concurrently either in whole or in part? ▪ Are all the essentials mentioned in this chapter included?
Resources	▪ How many people are needed for each of the tasks involved? ▪ How much time is required in relation to the number of people available for each task, or vice versa? ▪ How much budget is available in relation to all the tasks required, or vice versa? ▪ Is sufficient equipment (hardware and software) available?
Project management	▪ Who is going to be the overall project manager for the TBT programme? ▪ Have they got the appropriate skills and knowledge required, such as a good understanding of the overall process, an attention to detail; are they calm when things go wrong; can they solve problems quickly and effectively; can they lead and manage a large team of people; and are they able to stand back and see the whole picture on a regular basis? ▪ Does there need to be one sub-project manager or two – one to look after the instructional design and development and the other to manage all the other production tasks (graphics, audio and video, and programming)? ▪ At what stages does sign-off need to take place, and how many essential meetings with clients or sponsors are likely to be required, and at what stages?
Project definition and plan (PDP)	▪ Has a PDP been scheduled into the overall task list; if so, at what stage can it be prepared? ▪ Does the PDP consist of the following: an overview of the project, key objectives, aspects out of scope, main roles and responsibilities, a project plan showing tasks, those involved, start and end dates, a breakdown of costs and a risk analysis? ▪ Is the risk analysis comprehensive and realistic, and does it provide a rating for each risk shown alongside a suggested course of action should it be needed?

properly. Table 8 highlights some of the key issues to be addressed in order to achieve top-notch project planning and management.

If project planning and management are lacking, even to a small degree, then it is highly likely that the instructional design of the TBT programme will also be compromised to a directly proportional extent.

In brief

■ Owing to the nature of TBT, inadequacies in instructional design will usually be both expensive and time-consuming to put right.

■ In order to provide a high-quality TBT programme, the knowledge, skills and experience of instructional design are required to their greatest extent.

■ The essentials when producing either a generic or a bespoke TBT programme are:

  ❑ a needs analysis that defines any training required

  ❑ learning objectives that support the knowledge and skills (competences) required

  ❑ a profile of the target audience, segmented where necessary

  ❑ a 'blueprint' or an instructional strategy for the required training

  ❑ a briefing and specification document for the TBT programme to ensure that everyone involved works to the same criteria and guidelines

  ❑ a design prototype that ensures a conducive user interface is produced

  ❑ scripts or programme-ready materials

  ❑ high-quality project planning and management.

■ If any of the essentials are omitted, there will be a detrimental effect on the overall quality and effectiveness of the instructional design of the resulting TBT programme.

4

The Blueprint

Introduction

This chapter looks in detail at one of the essentials in instructional design: the production of a blueprint or instructional strategy. The importance of this document cannot be overestimated, because it really embodies in so many ways the instructional design of any training programme. Essentially, it is where the target audience's identified training needs are examined in detail to provide an overall plan for the look of the training programme.

Although there is no one specific way of producing an instructional strategy – or, come to that, any firm prescription as to what should be included – I shall cover the things that have worked well for me over the years. In doing so, I shall indicate why I think these aspects are important and how they can be handled for maximum effect. Also, it's vital at the outset to be clear about who the instructional strategy is for and who will need to sign it off. For example, is it for any or all of the following:

▌ a client or sponsor who is going to pay for the training programme

▌ an in-house training team, some or all of whom may be involved in the design, development and delivery of the resulting training

▌ an external supplier who will be involved in some or all of the design, development and delivery of the training

■ senior managers, line managers or training managers, all of whom have a vested interested in the training which is going to be produced?

As you work your way through this chapter try asking yourself:

■ Do I understand the importance of each aspect that has been described?'

■ What relevance has each aspect to me in my present situation?

■ Is this something that I or others do already or, if not, why not?

■ If I was going to produce something like this, what additional resources and skills would I need?

Before looking at each aspect in detail, here is a brief recap of the main headings that I like to see in an instructional strategy:

■ a description of the overall brief, including details of the target audience

■ a statement of the key aims and terminal objectives of the training programme

■ an overall structure and sequence of the training

■ a programme map showing what is available, at what stage and for whom

■ a description of the assessment strategy to be used

■ an outline of any evaluation strategy required

■ recommendations for delivering the training programme in relation to the most cost-effective media

■ details of elements, modules and sections that will go to make up the training programme

■ any additional information that might be required and from where, before any further work on the training programme can commence.

An overall brief

Now, although this part does not need to be of essay-type proportions, it is extremely helpful to all concerned if the instructional strategy starts with a cogent and succinct description of why the training programme is needed in the first place. There is no need to regurgitate the findings of the TNA or needs analysis at this point (although reference to it should be made), because all that is needed is to highlight why the training is needed and who it is for.

This is also the opportunity to set out the key, underpinning facts upon which the instructional design must be based. For example, you may want to mention some or all of the following:

- exactly who the training is for, eg by job title, job role, or other description
- exactly why the training is required, eg what needs it is required to meet
- what is known about the target audience that has to be taken into account, eg size, definite segments and their characteristics, general points such as the amount of time available for training, location, morale and attitudinal issues, special considerations
- any prerequisites that have to be taken into account, eg available budget, the date by when the training is required, the availability of training rooms, learning centres, equipment, etc.

Aims and objectives

There are some clear and important differences between aims and objectives so, because these will have an effect on various aspects of the instructional design, it is important not to confuse the one with the other. Setting out the key aims and terminal objectives for the training programme near the beginning of the instructional strategy helps to focus the reader's mind on what the training is aiming to provide and what knowledge and skills the user is supposed to acquire.

Target practice

As far as aims are concerned, they should be brief descriptions of what the training programme is hoping to achieve. When writing aims I always think of a target of some description, such as one used in archery, and then liken the training programme to the arrows in terms of what I, the instructional designer, am aiming to achieve. In this way I can easily produce statements along the lines of :

To introduce participants to new working procedures...

To enable participants to acquire the skills required to...

To show participants how to...

At this stage the aims do not need to be that specific, because this will come at a later stage in the instructional strategy. All that is needed is to look at the overall brief and to derive the key aims from this.

Getting terminal

When it comes to providing the key terminal objectives (which are statements concerning the main knowledge and skills that participants will be expected to master and to demonstrate), all you need to do is take a look at the competences identified and ascertain which are the main ones that need to be addressed by the training. Using these as your criteria you should then be able to produce the key terminal objectives, perhaps along these lines:

To describe the new working procedures...

To demonstrate the skills required to...

To demonstrate how to...

Once again, it's not necessary to specify the key learning objectives in great detail, because this will also be carried out at a later stage.

> If you want to check up on learning objectives, Chapter 3 will provide you with more information.

Making the difference work

The difference between aims and objectives can really be made to work for you because:

■ the aims will provide guidance on the overall thrust and direction of the training programme. They will also help you to focus on what really matters and to make sure that the overall approach is conducive to participants' achieving the key objectives.

■ the key terminal objectives will help you to focus on the most important learning outcomes and to make sure that all the relevant key subject matter or content is covered in the training programme. They will also help you in the next stage when you come to decide how the content should be structured and sequenced to achieve maximum learning effectiveness.

Overall structure and sequence

Whereas the foregoing can be likened to a taster before the main event, the main course now awaits. This is where the instructional design starts to take shape by creating something akin to a recipe for its production. The recipe, in this situation, provides the infrastructure for the rest of the instructional design and its development. It is therefore vital that the recipe not only contains all the right ingredients but that the method for using all these ingredients is also sound.

What is needed at this stage is to:

■ stand back and take a long, hard look at what needs to

be covered in terms of content (knowledge and skills) in the training programme

∎ think about an overall, logical sequence in which this content could be presented, taking into account the needs of the target audience, including any segments that have been identified

∎ sketch out some possible, workable sequences worth considering

∎ go back to the key aims and learning objectives and check these against your sketches – deleting any of the latter that you consider inadequate.

∎ think, impartially, about each of the sketches that remain in terms of how, as a user, you would feel about them – do they make sense, do they feel right, would they help you to master the objectives – or even ensure that you do?

∎ coalesce all the good, positive points into an overall structure and sequence for the training programme.

Honesty always pays

Well, so they say! I have to say that describing in detail how to structure and sequence the content of a training programme is not as straightforward as it might at first appear. The reason for this is that the process is, essentially, hard to break down into basic, easy-to-use and understandable steps. The reality is that much of the process relies on your having an intuitive understanding and feel for the way in which people learn – all of which is pretty hard to put into words, and can only be truly acquired through experience! However, some learning guidelines do exist that I, for one, have found to be extremely useful when structuring and sequencing content and that, to date, have never let me down.

How do people learn?

This question is fundamental to instructional design – indeed, *I cannot think of any more important question,* especially with regard to the various answers that it invariably generates! Even the most talented instructional designers will admit that if we knew exactly how people – in particular, adults – learn, then all would be relatively plain sailing. But there's the rub: the hard fact is that we really do not know for certain how adults learn, and it is largely because of this that so many of the elements of instructional design rely a lot on intuitive understanding.

Although there is a sound body of research into the way in which children learn, there is comparatively little with regard to adult learning. Some people talk about pedagogy (how children learn) and andragogy (how adults learn), because the distinction is an important one for them. I admit that I am one of these, for, having spent my career in helping both children and adults to learn, my experience tells me that adults do learn in different ways from those of children. However, having said that, some of the sound pedagogical research that we have available still has a part to play, for example when considering how people acquire and develop concepts in relation to the stage of conceptual development they have reached.

Learning styles

One of the most frequently heard terms when people are discussing instructional design, particularly in relation to TBT, is that of 'learning styles'. If I had a pound sterling for every time I had heard this term I would be quite a wealthy person! 'You must take into account their learning styles', instructional designers are advised almost on a regular basis, to the point that 'learning styles' have now become something of a mystical, unquestioned entity. But what exactly are learning styles, and do they hold any water when it comes to instructional design?

Before going any further, particularly if you are a believer in 'learning styles', I should point out that you may find what comes next somewhat divergent from a lot of mainstream opinion. However, my aim is to be neither disparaging nor contentious, but purely to take a critical look at what has become almost a given, and one with enormous implications for designing TBT. Indeed, the subject of learning styles is something that all instructional designers should consider and make up their own minds about.

Which model?

The first problem to be solved is which model of learning styles you should use – yes, there is more than one. Although some models are more popular or better-known than others, most of them are based on the consultant's stock-in-trade two-axis diagram with four neat learning styles, albeit with different titles. Now, immediately I ask myself, 'How come there is more than one model?' If the concept of learning styles was a given, then surely there would be some form of agreement about what these styles are? The existence of several models strongly suggests there is no common agreement about learning styles – unless, of course, you decide to ignore this inconvenience and attempt to take account of them all!

The other, and perhaps most important, issue to address is where exactly the research is upon which each of these models has been formulated. When the word 'research' is used, particularly in relation to any form of sound psychological research, it usually means that there exists a body of valid and reliable evidence collected in a methodical manner over many years and from a large and representative sample of the population. So, when it comes to the various models of learning styles it is important to ask where this type of research evidence is. If no one can provide such evidence then, again, it is quite reasonable to question the real value of any particular model.

A self-fulfilling prophecy?

The next thing to consider is what is likely to be involved if you do adopt a particular model of learning styles. The usual procedure is to give people a questionnaire to fill in so that you can determine their own learning style, the results of which are then fed back to each participant. Leaving aside the extremely serious issue concerning the basis on which these questionnaires are designed, imagine how you would feel to be told that you were an 'x' when it came to learning. I have actually witnessed people who were willingly participating in a training activity one moment, only to denounce its means of delivery a few minutes later after they had been told that they were a 'such and such'! It's a bit like telling someone that because they were born under the star sign Leo they are likely to be bossy, dominant, have leadership potential, be warm-hearted and so on! Sure, some may be, but equally well there may be many who are not.

I know that when it comes to learning I have some preferences in relation to how I go about this. For example, I may prefer to read about something first, think about it, and work it out in my own mind and internalise it before I decide what I should do next. Likewise, there are other occasions when I know that I shall need to try something out for myself if I am going to learn all about it, particularly when I am faced with something that I know at some point I shall have to show others I can actually do. Here the distinction between knowledge and skills is apparent once more: having a preference is one thing, but to insist on using it to meet all one's learning needs is quite another. So, although I may have a preference with regard to how I learn, I would not go as far as saying that I have a 'fixed' learning style that must be catered for every time I undertake some training. Of course when the results of their questionnaire are analysed you may find there are some people who have no particular preferred learning style, for which, I suppose, we should all be eternally grateful, because it shows that not all of us can be placed neatly into one of four little boxes!

Learning styles and TBT

The other important consideration, particularly in relation to TBT, is how to accommodate a target audience that has different learning styles irrespective of which model is being used. One solution, which in the majority of cases is completely impractical in terms of both cost and time, is to design four or five (if you want to please those who do not have a preferred style) different versions of the programme, each of which should satisfy a specific learning style. There have also been other attempts at solving this problem, such as building in some form of 'artificial intelligence' into programmes so that the latter can react 'intuitively' to the way in which the user starts to interact with it. However, once again, these solutions have proved to be both expensive and time-consuming, neither of which characteristics can be tolerated in most situations. More importantly, all this frantic endeavour, particularly as far as I am concerned, has somewhat missed the point about what learning is all about.

Isn't learning contextual?

As far as I am concerned, one of the most important things when considering how adults learn is to look at the learning in context, ie in terms of what it is that the person needs to learn and what they need to do with what they have learned. A colleague of mine used to tell this somewhat allegorical story of what can happen when someone clings to their preferred learning style while trying to fly in the face of their basic survival instincts:

Imagine this scene – a squad of new army recruits all lined up on the parade ground ready for a bit of 'square-bashing'. The regimental sergeant major, with his swagger stick tucked smartly under his arm, toe-caps you can see your face in and tunic buttons arranged in perfect vertical symmetry and all gleaming in the bright, early morning sunlight, barks an announcement to his 'trainees' that the objective for today is to learn how to present arms. In reality this is communicated to the recruits along these lines: 'Right, you miserable lot, by the time I've finished with you, you will all give me a perfect demonstration of how to present arms – and, pay attention, the word "mistake" is *not* in my vocabulary.'

At which point the RSM starts to go through his stock-in-trade training routine, only to be interrupted by one suicidal soul a few minutes later: 'Excuse me, regimental sergeant major, but this way of learning is not my preferred style. I learn best when I can go to the library and read a book on the subject. So, if it's okay with you, I'll go and do that now.' Now, although the RSM's reply is unprintable, the moral of this story is quite plain to see!

The context for learning can be found in the learning objectives, which is another good reason for taking the time to produce them. If an outcome is to demonstrate a skill or a procedure, then the means by which this is achieved must be fit for its purpose, the upshot of which is that theoretical approaches will not on their own be suitable, irrespective of how some people may prefer to learn.

Principles of adult learning

So what other help is available to an instructional designer when considering the structure and sequence of a training programme? Well, my choice lies in using some best-practice guidelines that set out the main principles of adult learning. These principles have arisen mainly from some of the work conducted over the years on andragogy, though most people will be able to identify with them quite easily.

Table 9 on page 64 lists the principles involved, along with a brief description of each.

Table 9

PRINCIPLES OF ADULT LEARNING

Principle	Description
Problem-centred	Most adults are motivated to learn when the training content is addressing a problem, such as something that they need to do better in the workplace, or when something new is going to be introduced that they have got to get to grips with. If people can see the relevance of what they are doing they are more likely to learn effectively.
Immediate application	It is also important that the content can be seen to have immediate application. Although some learning, such as gaining a qualification, can be regarded as having a high degree of deferred gratification attached to it, training is seen to be far more 'right here, right now'. If the content does not appear to have any immediate application, people can become bored, frustrated or disillusioned.
Build on previous experience	One of the main differences between children and adults is that the latter bring with them a considerable amount of experience. Even when something completely new needs to be learned it is extremely short-sighted to treat the recipients as 'empty vessels'. By building on what people know and can already do, you will help them feel valued and able to internalise their learning more easily.
Learner control	Another adult characteristic is the need to feel in control of what we are doing. Although at school we may have got used to being told when to learn, where to learn and how to learn, as adults we often resent this type of treatment. So by being put in control of their learning users often feel more empowered and motivated to learn.
Active participation	Both for children and adults, learning is not usually at its most effective when no form of participation is allowed. We need to try out most of the things we learn about, practise them in some way, have the opportunity to ask questions about them, and so on. Even the old method of lecturing, where the 'guru' stood and poured out his or her knowledge to a supposedly receptive audience, is now largely a thing of the past. You remember the saying, 'I do and I understand'?
Whole–Part– Whole learning	This is to do with how people build up important concepts and an overall picture or schema of a particular subject or area of content. Although not all people are the same, most people benefit from being presented with a complete picture, then moving to some detail in relation to a part of it,

	back to the whole picture again, and so on. The extent to which the subject itself should be broken down into component parts and the number of parts required depends on the nature of the content, its conceptual structure and its level of complexity.
Time on task	Now although there are some dubious statements made about how much time adults can concentrate for, and that content should always be broken up into extremely small chunks, the amount of time allocated to each task is nonetheless important. If the time allocated is too long, particularly where the relevance of the task is not that clear, people can easily become bored and 'switched-off', just as they will if they feel they are having to spend too long on something that does not justify it.
Clear instructions	Do you get infuriated when people don't tell you what they want you to do, or when they seem to be playing some kind of mind-game with you? If you do then you are a typical adult. This is why clear instructions are important, so that everyone knows what they are expected to do.
Check for understanding	Another aspect vital for learning is to provide people with the opportunity to check that they understand something they have learned. This means that at appropriate stages in a training programme users should be given a task or an opportunity to practise or apply what they should have just learned, whether this is in the form of knowledge or skills, or both.
Feedback	Imagine for one moment what it would feel like to complete a training programme where you received no feedback whatsoever. Wouldn't you hate it? I know I would. Most of us want, indeed demand, some form of feedback to know how well we are doing, and to know in what ways we need to improve if we are to master the learning objectives.
Different rates	We are all individuals, aren't we? This means that there is no way we can all be expected to learn at exactly the same rate or pace as one another. Any instructional designer who assumes that everyone can learn at the same rate and who does not cater for any differences is courting disaster.
Different ways	No, I am not talking about learning styles here! What I am talking about is the need to provide people with some choice and, where appropriate, different opportunities by means of which they can undertake their learning. This can start with letting people choose their own route through a training programme to providing different forms of additional support where needed.

All these principles should be considered not only when designing the overall structure and sequence of a training programme but also when it comes to detailing each part or component of that programme.

Mapping it out

If people don't know where they are going, have never been there before and so lack even the vaguest mental picture of the route, and no one has given them a map, then it's likely that a lot of them will get lost along the way. Exactly the same can be said in relation to a training programme: if some sort of map is not provided, then all those who have a part to play in the design, development and delivery of the programme will probably find it difficult to form an overview – as will those on the receiving end.

For all those involved in the production of a training programme it is important to have a similar overview of what is involved. So, instead of expecting people to form their own, and possibly highly idiosyncratic, overview by piecing together in some way all the various elements, modules and sections described later on in the instructional strategy, a map or flowchart of what is involved will ensure that everyone is seeing pretty much the same sort of thing. As far as participants are concerned, the same map can be incorporated into the training programme in some way at an early stage so that people can see what is involved and get a good feel for the look and shape of what they are about to encounter.

Route planning

As is well known, getting from A to B can involve a number of different but equally viable routes. This can also apply to a training programme, in particular when TBT or other forms of distance learning are in the frame. When a training programme is, in effect, handed over to someone to use at a time and place of their own choosing and to manage as they see fit, it's of immense value to be given a good idea of the various routes to take through the training, and of the way that links between the various parts of the training actually work.

When an instructional designer has structured and sequenced the content of a training programme, particularly one that has to cater for different learning needs and in which the overall sequence does not have to be linear or hierarchical, they may very well have produced a map of the programme that shows possible routes for different segments of the target audience, as well as how parts of the programme link together. If they have, then that's just dandy, because without any further ado they can include this in their instructional strategy; if not, then they should get a-mapping!

Figure 2 on page 68 shows a hypothetical example of what I mean by a programme map. It shows in particular what a programme map might look like: an overview of the whole event, plus the routes that can be taken and how some of its parts link together.

Assessment and evaluation

Although assessment and evaluation are often mentioned in the same breath, as far as I am concerned there is a huge difference between them.

- *Assessment* is where individuals are tested or test themselves in order to see how much they have learned and to what extent they have mastered any stated learning objectives. Assessment can be formative (ie in the form of feedback) and summative (ie at the end of a module or programme to test whether mastery has been achieved).

- *Evaluation* is where the training programme is tested, using data from either the total number of users or a representative sample of the total population, to see how far the programme has been effective. Evaluation

Figure 2

PROGRAMME MAP

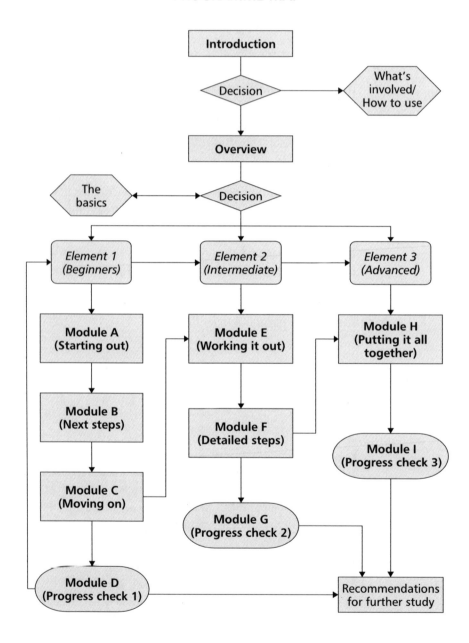

can also be formative (ie providing diagnostic data that can be used to improve the programme) and summative (ie at the end of the programme to prove that it has brought about the changes it was designed to achieve).

Assessment

Some organisations have a specific strategy when it comes to assessment. For example, it may be policy that all training programmes contain both formative and summative assessment, that all participants be measured against specific learning objectives or performance criteria, and that all assessment data be captured, stored and fed back to all participants and their line managers. Where such a strategy exists, reference should be made to it in the instructional strategy and then, where appropriate, details provided with regard to how the strategy will be implemented in the training programme.

In the absence of any assessment strategy, the instructional designer should give careful consideration to what can be achieved within both time and budget. For example, it should be a given that formative assessment must be included and that mastery of the learning objectives be tested. Other considerations, particularly in relation to bespoke training programmes, are likely to involve how the assessment data can be collected (eg manually or electronically), how they can be stored and retrieved (eg via an existing student or performance management system), and how the collated or analysed data can be fed back to all those who need them in a form that fits into and supports any other personnel-type systems, such as appraisals and personal development plans.

At this stage it's not necessary to start thinking in any great detail about exactly how the learning objectives can be measured: this will come a little later on in the instructional strategy. However, I will say one thing about assessment at this point: all too often it proves to be the weakest part of many a training programme by incorporating poorly designed test items incapable of measuring what they are supposed to be measuring and bearing very little or no relationship to the content covered in the programme!

Evaluation

Pretty much the same applies here as it does to assessment. In other words, if there is an evaluation strategy already in place, refer to it in the instructional strategy. If not, then there are some basic questions you should answer before jumping to the conclusion that evaluation is a jolly good thing and should be included in the training programme. Table 10 lists these questions and describes why each one is important.

Evaluation is a large and complex subject, which means that there is a lot more to it than just answering the six questions provided in Table 10. Although these questions will help you to formulate an evaluation strategy and an overall methodology, if you want to find out more about the subject take a look at another book in this series – *Evaluating Training* by Peter Bramley (CIPD, 1996).

Deciding which media to use

At this point you should be in a position to describe which type of media can be used to 'deliver' the training programme. This may be a clear-cut decision or it may be necessary to provide some alternative solutions along with their relative costs and time-scales in order for other people to make the final decision. In making the initial recommendation it is necessary to consider the strengths and weaknesses of each medium in relation to the learning objectives, the content or subject matter in question, and available resources.

Table 10

EVALUATION?

Question	Importance
Why *does the training programme need to be evaluated?*	In the first place it's essential that you know why you are evaluating training – is it to show that it is cost-effective, provides added value, justifies budgets, massages people's egos?
Who *is the evaluation for?*	In ascertaining the 'why' you also need to ascertain the 'who'. Exactly who needs or wants to be included – who are the stakeholders with a vested interest in the outcomes of the evaluation?
What *is it they need to know?*	Having established the 'why' and the 'who' it is then necessary to establish precisely what it is these people need or want to know – you will then have all the information required to produce a brief evaluation strategy.
How *can the evaluation be conducted?*	As well as providing some strategic direction for the evaluation, it is also helpful at this stage to include some methodological aspects. *How* will the data required be gathered: what measurements will be required and what tools will be needed?
When *can it take place?*	*When* will the tools be used and measurements made: before, during or after the training programme?
Where *does it need to be carried out?*	*Where* will the tools be used and the measurements made – in the training programme itself, in the workplace, in the training room or learning centre?

Now, if this all sounds somewhat complex and analytical, possibly along the lines of a distorted form of 'whodunnit' ('Well, I reckon it must be distance learning with TBT in a learning centre'), then let me try to reassure you. In most situations it is extremely likely that the decision will be quite clear-cut and that you will have already started to develop a good picture early on in the process of designing your instructional strategy. For example, if the learning objectives and the subject matter are concerned with using a new computer system or computer-based processes, it is more than likely that the training media will have to be some form of TBT. In such cases it is then just a matter of backtracking and justifying your initial hunches.

TBT *rules!*

Now because this book is about instructional design in relation to TBT there are no prizes for guessing what comes next: surprise, surprise, 'It is recommended that the main medium for delivering the training in question is TBT.' Apologies if you were thinking up to this point that I had slightly lost my way, but I had to make sure that all the prerequisites had been covered and I had demonstrated that the decision to use a particular medium is not always straightforward. If in any doubt, just bear in mind this sobering little thought, as penned by one W. S. Gilbert (he of 'Gilbert and Sullivan' fame): 'Things are seldom what they seem/Skim milk masquerades as cream.' So very true, especially when it comes to TBT, because, in essence, no training delivery medium is ever what it truly seems! Whatever the situation, learning needs or content, it's always a question of selecting the most suitable means by which people can learn most effectively.

> Do you feel clear in your own mind about the strengths and weaknesses of TBT? Yes? Then it's time to get down to the nitty-gritty. No? Then it might help to revisit 'TBT in action' in Chapter 2 (pages 17-27).

Now it's down to the details

What happens next is like putting all the fleshy bits onto a superbly crafted skeleton. Because this part of an instructional strategy will become a main reference source for all those involved with writing the scripts or PRMs for the TBT programme, it's very important to make sure that it contains all the necessary details to enable each writer to produce high-quality and instructionally sound scripts. I find the following breakdown and list of headings both useful and workable for fleshing out the elements, modules and sections previously identified when structuring and sequencing the training programme:

- title, aims and objectives
- content
- time for average study
- teaching/learning points
- use of assessment
- specific treatment.

Title, aims and objectives

Each element, module and section should be given a specific name or title, preferably one that describes as succinctly as possible the content or the aims to be covered. Following the title, the aim or aims are stated, and then the terminal and enabling objectives. Although this sounds quite neat and tidy, you may need to flex this layout a little, particularly where a module has a number of different sections or an element contains a number of different modules. For example, you may want to place some of the aims and objectives in different parts of the overall structure so that the hierarchy of what you are trying to achieve is clear to see. Figure 3 on page 74 shows how this could be done.

Content

Under this heading can be placed a list of all the main content to be covered in the element, module or section. It should be possible to generate this list from the content or subject matter that appears in the terminal and enabling objectives.

Figure 3

STATING AIMS AND OBJECTIVES

Element 1

Title: The Overall Title

Aim: To provide the overall aim for the element

Objectives: To describe the main, terminal objectives for the element.

> **Module:**   The First One
>
> **Aim:**   To provide the aim(s) of the module
>
> **Objectives:** To describe the terminal objectives of the module.
>
>> **Section:**   The First Part
>>
>> **Aim:**   To provide the aims of the section
>>
>> **Objectives:** To describe the terminal objectives of the section and all its enabling objectives.
>>
>> **Content:**   ....
>>
>> **Time:**   ....
>>
>> **and so on.........**

Repeat the above for all remaining sections in the first module and then go on to the next module and all its sections and so on until the first element is complete. Start all over again with the next element. Ensure an adequate supply of liquid refreshement is available throughout!

Time for average study

It is extremely helpful, particularly to scriptwriters, to provide a notional number of study minutes that the section or module is likely to take the average user to complete. Some people swear by timing the amount of TBT required in terms of a specific number of frames, for example where two frames are equal to one minute, or to using some other strange or particularly esoteric type of formula. Although the former was quite an acceptable approach when TBT consisted mainly of text and graphics, now that multimedia are being used extensively one frame can be extremely different from another in terms of its volume. As an instructional designer I find it is more helpful to say, for example, that a section should take the average user five minutes (meaning that others may take less or more), so that when I put my scriptwriting hat on I can then translate this quite easily into providing approximately five minutes' worth of TBT, including the time required for all the interactions as well as for listening to audio, watching video, looking at graphics and reading text.

Teaching/learning points

Here it is a matter of listing the main teaching or learning points to be addressed. This part will provide the writers with a most useful checklist when they are scripting the particular section or module. The main teaching or learning points can usually be ascertained by taking another look at the content to be covered in the section or module in relation to the learning objectives – although it may be desirable to flesh the teaching/learning points out a little at this stage to ensure that they are both clear and comprehensive.

Use of assessment

Reference here should be made to the type of assessment required (eg formative or summative) and how it should be handled. *Formative* feedback is likely to be on an ongoing basis throughout the section or module to provide a check on the mastery of the enabling objectives, whereas *summative* assessment should be used to assess the mastery of the terminal objectives at appropriate stages. It is also helpful at this stage to make some suggestions as to the type of assessments that could be used by the scriptwriters, such as question and answer, multiple-choice items, calculations, demonstrating a course of action, the use of simulations and so on. Inspection of the teaching or learning points in conjunction with the learning objectives should provide valuable clues as to the most suitable types of assessment items for the module or section.

Specific treatment

Finally, it may be necessary to mention any features, such as the use of video, required in the section or module, along with any specific treatment of the content. For example, the needs analysis may have thrown up an issue to be handled in a particularly sensitive or, alternatively, dogmatic manner. It may also be necessary to specify the use of a case study or a specific order in which the teaching or learning points should be presented. Any specific treatment that relates only to the section or module in question should be described at this point.

Any additional information required?

Can there possibly be anything else? Probably not, but, just in case there is, this is the place to mention it. I find this heading particularly useful for mentioning those things where I know more information still needs to be provided by the client or subject-matter expert – for example, if further details are still to be supplied about how some segments of the target audience will be required to use parts of a new procedure or system, or where there is the possibility that some content may need to be added or deleted after further discussion. In this way you can produce a useful *aide-mémoire* and checklist for all those concerned.

In brief

■ A blueprint or an instructional strategy is an indispensable part of designing any training programme.

■ Although there is no definitive framework to use for producing an instructional strategy, it is helpful to include:

☐ an overall brief and description of the target audience

☐ the key aims and terminal objectives

☐ the overall structure and sequence of the training

☐ a programme map showing an overview of the training, any different routes that can be taken and how modules etc link together

☐ the assessment strategy to be used, along with (where relevant) the same for evaluation

☐ how the training programme will be delivered, or recommendations for different media or combinations thereof

☐ a detailed description of the various parts of the training programme (eg elements, modules, sections)

☐ any additional information still required.

■ It is helpful to remember that there are some important differences between aims and objectives, and to break down the latter into terminal and enabling objectives for use later on.

■ The use of best-practice guidelines in relation to how adults learn will prove to be very useful when structuring and sequencing the content.

■ Due consideration should be given to assessment, and to how mastery of the learning objectives will be measured, because this is often one of the weakest parts of many training programmes, particularly TBT programmes, where so much potential for assessment exists.

■ The details provided of the various parts of the TBT programme will be an invaluable guide for all those involved in writing or scripting the PRMs.

5 Producing Briefs

Introduction

The production of any TBT programme – even a really small one – will inevitably require the involvement of a number of people. Depending on the type and size of the programme, along with the multimedia features to be incorporated, some or all of the following people shown in Table 11 on page 80 will be involved in producing the final version of most bespoke or generic TBT programmes.

All of this means in practice quite a few people fulfilling different job roles. In addition, other people will need to know something about what is going on, for example tutors and any other support staff, especially if the TBT programme is to be delivered online to users, so that they feel involved and committed to the project. Just imagine what could happen if all these people were left to their own devices and that all they had to go on was an instructional strategy! For sure, they would have most of what they needed to know but there would still be one vital piece of information missing: a TBT 'hymn sheet' – in other words, a briefing and specification document.

In this chapter I am going to open up a typical briefing and specification document to have a look at the sort of information it can contain. Just as with an instructional strategy, there is no set format or structure for such a document, so I have pieced together all the various bits of information that I think are useful and that, as an

Table 11

PRODUCING TBT PROGRAMMES

Area of responsibility	Job function
Management	Project manager Sub-project managers: ∎ Design and development ∎ Production
Design and development	Instructional designer(s) Course or scriptwriter(s) – these are often the instructional designers, unless the programme is extremely large.
Production	Graphic designers Programmers Audio artists Audio recording and editing producers Video producers
Quality control	Client/sponsor Subject matter expert(s) Project manager Instructional designer Evaluators

instructional designer, I would wish to communicate to all those involved in the production of a TBT programme.

> As you go through this chapter you may find it helpful to think about:
>
> ∎ how each of the areas mentioned relate to instructional design
>
> ∎ what impact each area will have on instructional design
>
> ∎ what would happen if this information was not made available to all those involved in producing a TBT programme.

Brief rules of engagement

The first area to cover is what might be deemed a brief description of the general approach to be taken in relation to using text, audio, graphics, animation, video and interactions. Essentially what the instructional designer is doing here is to provide the standards and guidelines for each of these multimedia features. Figure 4 on page 82 shows how this might look.

Now, obviously, this is only an example to show you just some of the standards and guidelines that can be included at this point. What is actually included must, of course, be in direct relationship to the actual TBT programme in question. However, what is important here is that what is included relates directly to the quality of the learning or, in other words, the instructional design.

> Take another look at what's been included in Figure 4. How many of the standards or guidelines shown here do you think relate directly to various aspects of learning?
>
> If you have used a TBT programme at some point, do you think that the programme you used was designed using standards and guidelines along the lines suggested? If not, what was the overall effect?

Laying down the standards

If you are preparing this part of a briefing and specification document or are checking one that has already been produced, it's a good idea to look for the following, as shown in Table 12 on page 83.

Figure 4

General Approach:

The general features of the TBT programme will be as follows:

- Easy to use, consisting of a main menu and basic navigation buttons.
- User interaction will be built in wherever possible and appropriate. Interaction will be mainly in the form of data entry, feedback questions and responses to mini case studies.
- Each module will use a combination of text, audio, graphics (including animation where relevant) and short video clips.
- Text will be used to summarise the main points provided in the audio, to confirm instructions and to provide feedback. Users will control when they move on after a text box has appeared.
- Each module will conclude with a text summary of the main learning points.
- Audio will consist of a narrator (female voice) who will guide users through the TBT programme. In addition a tutor (male voice) will be used to provide explanations in relation to various learning points.
- Graphics will be a mixture of pictures, drawings, diagrams and cartoons.
- Video clips will be used to introduce to users six specific customers, each of whom will have different requirements that users will need to respond to appropriately.
- The TBT programme will encourage first-time users to work through the learning material in a sequential order, but the programme will be designed to allow all users access to any module or part of a module (section) as they wish.
- The overall impact of the TBT programme in terms of the design of the user interface, the use of text, audio and graphics will be warm, friendly and encouraging.

Table 12

GENERAL APPROACH

Aspect	Look for
General	Comments about the general look and feel of the TBT programme, how it is intended to be used, any particular features that will be required.
Text	How text will be used in the TBT programme, eg to support audio, to summarise points, to provide feedback etc.
Audio	How audio will be used in the TBT programme, what voices will be used and what roles will be played.
Graphics	What type of graphics will be used in the TBT programme and any specific restrictions on or instructions for their use.
Animations	When animations should be used and how they should be used, eg moving diagrams, cartoons replacing video sequences.
Video	How and when any video sequences should be used, the characters involved and the role they play.
Interaction	The type and range of interactions to be included in the TBT programme.

Seamanship

Navigating, or finding your way, around a TBT programme by interacting with the user interface is a vital component in terms of learning. Not only does the choice of precisely what functions are included need careful consideration but it is also very important that all the functions selected work on a consistent basis throughout the programme. Figure 5 on page 84 shows some of the different navigation buttons that can often be found in TBT programmes.

Figure 5

FUNCTION AND NAVIGATION BUTTONS

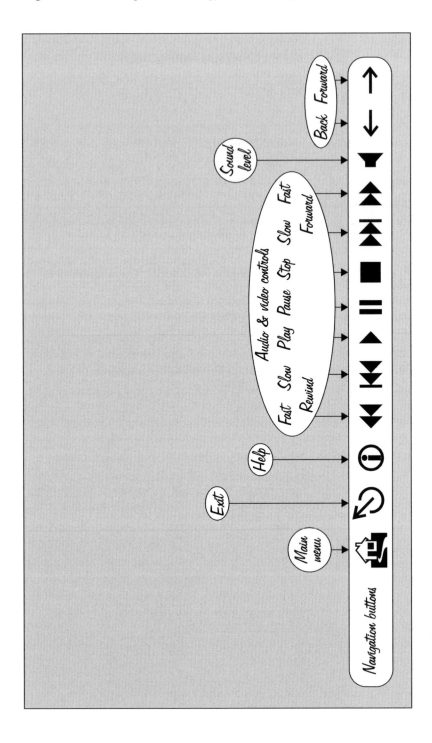

Figure 6 is an example of what can be included in a briefing and specification document in relation to how the selected function and navigation buttons will be used.

Figure 6

Use of Function and Navigation Buttons

Main Menu: this takes users back to the main menu, where the list of modules is displayed.

Module Menu: this takes users to a section or sub-section menu.

Search: this lets users search for a specific topic. If the topic has various aspects, users will be given a number of options from which to choose. Clicking on an option will take them to the relevant part of the TBT programme.

Help: this gives users help on various aspects of the programme, ranging from navigation to technical issues.

Glossary: this will provide users with a brief description/explanation of the main terms, arranged in alphabetical order, that are used throughout the programme.

Bookmark: this lets users mark a specific screen so that they can return to it when they restart the programme or when they want to return to a specific screen.

Retrieve: this lets users go back to their bookmarked page.

Back: this will take users back to the start of the previous sequence. A sequence is defined as the block of screens users go through before having to click on the forward button.

Replay: this will replay the current screen and associated components.

Forward: this will take users to the start of the next sequence/frame.

Exit: this takes users out of the programme – users can also keep clicking on the menu button until they get back to the main menu, where they can click on the Exit button – they will always be asked if they do want to exit and, if so, whether they want to bookmark the current screen first.

Checklist: each module has a checklist of key learning points. For handy reference these can be printed out by clicking on the print button when users are in a checklist screen.

Although a number of function and navigation buttons might be given different names, such as 'quit' or 'exit', and a variety of different appearances, essentially many of the basic functions are pretty much the same in most TBT programmes. Table 13 lists some of the things to be considered when thinking about navigation functionality.

Table 13

FUNCTION AND NAVIGATION BUTTONS

Consideration	Likely solution
How many buttons will be required, and where should they be located on the screen?	Essential buttons will be those that let people move forward or backward. A menu button will be required so that users can go back to the main menu at any time. Users should also be allowed to replay the current screen at any time without having to go back a set number of frames. Letting users bookmark and then retrieve a screen at any time, particularly after they have exited the programme, is also a very useful feature. A print button may also be needed if a screen or part of a screen has to be printed out for later use. As most navigation will be undertaken by using a mouse, tracker ball or track pad of some description, it is helpful – especially for left-handed users – to place all navigation buttons at the bottom of the screen.
How can users be informed about how much of the TBT programme they have completed?	A progress bar can appear on each screen to show users exactly how much of a module or section they have completed at any given point. On menu screens any icons used alongside each menu item can be completely or partly filled in, as appropriate. Alternatively a colour scheme could be used, such as green for uncompleted, amber for partly completed and red for completed.
How will users know that a button or a part of the screen is active?	The cursor needs to change shape to show this, or the button can flash or become highlighted. A common convention is for the usual pointer to change into the shape of a hand, in much the same way that it does when highlighting a link on an Internet website.
How easy should it be to exit a TBT programme at any point?	Ideally, users should be able to exit a TBT programme at any time, because it can be extremely frustrating to have to wait to reach a specific point or have to click your way back through several layers until you get to

	the exit button. However, the exit button should not be activated immediately, just in case the user clicks on it accidentally: there should always be a check question before the exit function is executed.
What additional help or performance support features will be needed?	A help button is a very useful feature, which can be searched by keyword or by pointing to a specific area of the screen – much in the same way as the help function works in Microsoft Word™. However, designing a good help facility is no small task and will add to the time and costs involved in producing the programme. Another useful feature is a glossary of some kind, so that users can check up on the definitions of technical words and phases at any time.

Don't use that tone of voice with me!

Three aspects of instructional design that definitely need standards applied to them are the style, tone and pitch of the text, audio, graphics and video. In deciding what these standards should be, due consideration needs to be given to the profile of the target audience and to any segments that may have been defined. Figure 7 on page 88 is an example of the sort of thing that can appear under these three headings.

Although each of these – style, tone and pitch – are related, there are also clear and important differences between each. In some circumstances, such as when a large number of scriptwriters are involved, it may be necessary to provide some worked examples to illustrate the standards required.

> If you have used a few TBT programmes in the past, try casting your mind back to think about the style, tone and pitch used and how you reacted to them: was it a pleasurable experience, did anything grate on you, did you feel comfortable and encouraged?

It's important to recognise that all of us can be irritated by what a person says and how he or she says it. For example, one of my main bugbears is when a TBT

Figure 7

STYLE, TONE AND PITCH

Style:
In relation to the video and accompanying audio, the style used should be in line with the way in which the various characters are likely to speak. Depending on who is speaking (eg manager, representative, customers) this should reflect normal speaking styles. Because each customer, with the exception of Mrs White, appears only once, a personality style for each has been created (see page 00) which should be maintained throughout all the video clips.

The narrator and the tutor should both have a friendly, warm and clear style. Text, when used, should be precise, matter of fact, reinforcing and friendly. Graphics should be real, believable and suitable.

Tone:
The overall tone should be warm, helpful, friendly, encouraging and inviting. It should make users feel wanted and important, and that nothing is too much trouble. Humour should be used wherever relevant, creating a sense of enjoyment – and that this is a good place in which to work. In no way should the tone be patronising.

Pitch:
The overall pitch should be suitable for the target audience, ie mature individuals who have initiative and get up and go, who are motivated and keen to learn, and who may bring with them previous experience of the jobs into which they are to go.

programme narrator or tutor says, 'Now, let's look at...' or 'Now we'll take a look at...'! Both of these remind me of a somewhat bossy and patronising nurse saying, 'Now, how are we today?' Well, maybe that's just me for you, but I bet I'm not alone in being irritated by this particular style of speech. The best thing to do, if there is any possibility that some of the target audience could be made up of people like me, is to err on the side of caution and to make sure that such phrases are avoided.

Chartered Institute of Personnel and Development

Customer Satisfaction Survey

*We would be grateful if you could spend a few minutes answering these questions and return the postcard to CIPD. <u>Please use a black pen to answer.</u> **If you would like to receive a free CIPD pen, please include your name and address.*** IPD MEMBER Y/N

....

1. Title of book ....

2. Date of purchase: month .... year ....

3. How did you acquire this book?
☐ Bookshop   ☐ Mail order   ☐ Exhibition   ☐ Gift   ☐ Bought from Author

4. If ordered by mail, how long did it take to arrive:
☐ 1 week   ☐ 2 weeks   ☐ more than 2 weeks

5. Name of shop .... Town... Country............

6. Please grade the following according to their influence on your purchasing decision with 1 as least influential: (please tick)

	1	2	3	4	5
Title					
Publisher					
Author					
Price					
Subject					
Cover					

7. On a scale of 1 to 5 (with 1 as poor & 5 as excellent) please give your impressions of the book in terms of: (please tick)

	1	2	3	4	5
Cover design					
Paper/print quality					
Good value for money					
General level of service					

8. Did you find the book:
Covers the subject in sufficient depth   ☐ Yes   ☐ No
Useful for your work   ☐ Yes   ☐ No

9. Are you using this book to help:
☐ In your work ☐ Personal study   ☐ Both   ☐ Other (please state)

Please complete if you are using this as part of a course

10. Name of academic institution...

11. Name of course you are following? ....

12. Did you find this book relevant to the syllabus? ☐ Yes ☐ No ☐ Don't know

Thank you!

To receive regular information about CIPD books and resources call 020 8263 3387.

Any data or information provided to the CIPD for the purposes of membership and other Institute activities will be processed by means of a computer database or otherwise. You may, from time to time, receive business information relevant to your work from the Institute and its other activities. If you do not wish to receive such information please write to the CIPD, giving your full name, address and postcode. The Institute does not make its membership lists available to any outside organisation.

1795/05/00

2

BUSINESS REPLY SERVICE
Licence No WD 1019

Publishing Department

Chartered Institute of Personnel and Development

CIPD House

Camp Road

Wimbledon

London

SW19 4BR

Achilles' heel

All too often, assessment can be the Achilles' heel of a TBT programme. No matter how many standards or conventions are defined, if scriptwriters are unable to select the most appropriate type of assessment test item (multiple-choice, matching, true/false etc) or fail to design an appropriate test that truly measures both the enabling and terminal learning objectives, the end result will be an invalid or unreliable test. It cannot therefore be stressed enough that scriptwriters must also be experts in assessment test design and development. Assuming that the scriptwriters are up to the task, Figure 8 shows the sort of thing that can be included in a briefing and specification document.

Figure 8

Assessment:

Formative assessment will be built in to the modules as and when appropriate, in particular when inputting data into the various fields on each simulated screen. Formative assessment will also take the form of asking users questions to check their understanding and knowledge. In all cases users will be told whether they carried out the correct action or supplied the correct answer and, if not, they will be given appropriate assistance.

Summative assessment takes place in Module X – the last module. This will consist of a number of valid test items designed to measure the mastery of each learning objective. Feedback will be provided when users get an item wrong, so that they can judge whether or not they need to repeat a module or section. Users will be given their overall score along with an appropriate comment in terms of mastery and any suggested areas for re-study.

Assessing assessment

There are also some important things to consider when deciding on the overall approach to assessment; these can also be included in the briefing and specification document if they have not been mentioned in the instructional strategy. Table 14 answers some of the questions that may need to be considered at this point.

Table 14

ASSESSMENT CRITERIA

Question	Answer
Does a pre-test have to contain different test items from a post-test?	No, it doesn't. Exactly the same items can be used for both, because the whole idea is to measure mastery of the learning objectives, and therefore it does not matter whether people are provided with feedback that allows them to memorise the correct answer – provided, that is, they know why the answer is correct, which comes back again to the correct choice of test items! Because one aspect of a reliable test is the extent to which all the items correlate with one another (inter-item correlation), using the same test items makes sense, otherwise twice as many items will need to be designed, increasing the amount of time and hence the cost of this aspect.
Is it important to provide feedback in a post-test?	I think wherever possible it is. The only time I would think twice is where the feedback might help in answering any future test items. At a basic level people should be told whether they got the item correct or not. If they get it wrong then a really nice add-on is to explain why their answer wasn't correct – this is a particularly useful feature when multiple-choice items are used, although once again this does increase the amount of time required to design and programme the test.
Should users be allowed to repeat a post-test?	Why not? We are talking about mastery here, not a one-chance-type lottery! Also, people will vary with regard to whether they want to take the post-test again straight away or whether they first need to follow any recommendations for re-study.

How detailed should formative assessment be?	Basically, as detailed as possible. Just telling people 'No, that's wrong' is really unhelpful. Certainly, tell them nicely that they are wrong, but then tell them why they were wrong so that next time they will be right!
How flashy does the assessment have to be?	Not a lot. Above all, avoid any temptation to use a clapping sound when the answer is correct and a kind of 'bong' sound when they are wrong – basically because after a while this can become immensely irritating, apart from the fact that it is intensely patronising! A tick or a cross is okay, or some other kind of immediate visual response, plus some appropriate words either in text or audio format.

Now, that's what I call a script

Irrespective of the number of scriptwriters involved, one of the most important things to set out in a briefing and specification document is the layout for the programme-ready materials (or PRMs, as they are often called). In particular, standards or conventions in relation to the nomenclature, interactions and instructions to programmers should be defined and stated clearly. Once again, there is no one particular way in which to do this; in my time I have encountered many variations and layouts. Figure 9 on page 92 shows an example PRM layout that I have found to be a most satisfactory way to go about things. Don't worry if the layout doesn't make that much sense to you at this stage, because all will be explained in Table 15, which follows the example layout.

Figure 9

EXAMPLE PRM

Frame Number: 01.01.010

Instructions:
On entry

Graphic:
01.01.010a   Description etc.

Audio N:
01.01.010a   Script.

Text:
01.01.010a   Description etc.

Instructions:
(Place here any instructions to the programmer.)

  Graphic:
  01.01.010b   Description etc.

  Audio:
  01.01.010b   Script.

  Text:
  01.01.010b   Text.

Interaction:
If user...then... > Frame 01.01.020.
If else...
Audio:
01.01.010c   Script.
> Frame 01.01.020.

If else other than ...., instructions.
Text:
01.01.010c   Text.
When... > Frame 01.01.020.

FRWD: *> 01.01.020 (and/or)*
BACK: *> 01.01.010*

It's all in the script

In my experience the most important thing about the layout used for the PRMs is that it should be something everyone can get their head around – scriptwriters, clients or sponsors, subject-matter experts, graphic designers and programmers. It should tell the story as clearly and easily as possible so that, as others read the script, they can visualise exactly what is intended.

Table 15 lists some of the important features that should appear in all PRMs.

Table 15

PRMs EXPLAINED

Feature	Importance
Frames	TBT essentially consists of a number of frames, each of which should be given a distinct identity. In Figure 9, 01.01.010 could mean Module 1, Section 1, Frame 010 (ie the first frame). The next frame would be 01.01.020, and so on. If at some point additional frames need to be added, there is plenty of scope for this – 011, 012 etc. If Module 1 consists of several sections, then the next section will start at 01.02.010.
Assets	Each asset (graphic, text, audio, video) should have its own unique identifier, because this makes programming and editing a lot easier. This means that on each occasion an asset is used it is shown as a separate entity. When different voices are used for the audio or different people in a video clip, it's a good idea to place a code letter such as 'N' for narrator after the asset's name, so that everyone is quite clear about who is involved at any particular point.
Nomenclature	The nomenclature used for the assets follows that of the frames, except that the letters a, b, c, d etc are used as a suffix. So, in Frame 01.01.010 the first graphic asset is 01.01.010a, the second graphic is 01.01.010b and so on. The same goes for the audio, text and video, ie the first piece of audio is 01.01.010a, the second piece of audio is 01.01.010b etc. In this way, every single asset used in a frame can be identified easily.

(continued on page 94)

Instructions	There will be times when the scriptwriters need to provide some 'instructions' to the programmers, graphic designers or video production team. These may be firm instructions that relate directly to the instructional design, for example the timing of text bullet points to coincide with various parts of the audio, or they may be suggestions, such as rough ideas or requirements for graphics where the scriptwriter wants the person concerned to exercise his or her creative talent. If, for whatever reason, a scriptwriter's instructions prove to be unworkable, then the person to whom they are directed should discuss possible alternatives with the scriptwriter concerned; otherwise the instructional design can easily be compromised.
Interactions	Whenever the scriptwriter wants the user to interact in some way with the TBT programme, instructions to this effect should appear in the PRMs. One way of doing this is shown in Figure 9 – starting with 'If user does...then...', 'If else...'. The interactions provided can relate to moving on to a specific frame, to moving on to another asset or to providing help or feedback should the user not perform the desired interaction. The main thing to ensure is that all eventualities have been covered so that the user is not left high and dry, unable to move on. (Chapter 6 deals with this key feature of TBT programmes in more detail.)
Links	Each frame must be linked to another frame, even if the link is back to the main menu: a frame can't just end and be left hanging in mid-air. At the end of each frame, unless specified already in the final interaction for that frame, instructions need to be given as to what will happen when the user clicks on forward or back.
Overall structure	Each module should be self-contained and clearly marked with a separate front cover as shown in Figure 10 (below). On this sheet any further breakdown of the module (such as sections) can also be shown, along with the average study time. It is also helpful to include somewhere a version number and the date/time when the PRM was created in order to keep track of later versions and to ensure that everyone is working from the latest script.
Production	Obviously, hand-written PRMs will be extremely time-consuming to produce and to edit, so it important that all scriptwriters are comfortable with using a proprietary word-processing package such as Microsoft Word™. The instructional designer should provide a pro forma or template for the PRMs that all scriptwriters will then use to produce their scripts. In this way uniformity is established, and the scriptwriters themselves are free to get on with what is really important: the production of creative and instructionally sound PRMs.

Figure 10

PRM FRONT COVER

Company – Overall Title of TBT Programme   Module 01: Title

OVERALL TITLE OF TBT PROGRAMME

Module 00: Title

(No subsections) or
- **Section 1:   Title**
- **Section 2:   Title**
- **Section 3:   Title**
- **Section 4:   Title**
- **Section x: etc**

Approximate time for users to complete = x minutes.

[FileName] [Version: x]   [Date/Time]   Page: x

> If at this point you want to know more about producing PRMs, go to Chapter 7.

Editorial scruples

The one last thing that you may need to include in a briefing and specification document is some specific editorial guidelines and conventions. The template PRM will provide some guidance, but it is highly likely that additional information about some aspects of the instructional design and the nature of any instructions etc will also be needed. Figure 11 shows an example of what I mean.

Once again, this is only an example of what can be provided under the heading of editorial guidelines and conventions. Although it might be possible to have a fairly standard document, for example when a series of TBT programmes are being produced and they need to look and feel consistent as far as the user is concerned, it is usually necessary for the instructional designer to produce a specific document for each programme. The key is to keep this part as brief as possible so that the scriptwriters don't spend all their time referring back to it. This means that, although all the main points should be covered, it is not necessary to try to dot every 'i' and cross every 't'!

In brief

■ Because a number of people, each fulfilling different roles, will be involved in producing a TBT programme, it is essential that they are all conforming to the same standards, conventions, guidelines and specifications. To achieve this, a briefing and specification document is required on which the instructional designer should take the lead and be responsible for its production.

■ Such a document should contain details in relation to:

☐ the overall general approach

☐ the use of function and navigation buttons

☐ style, pitch, and tone

☐ assessment

Figure 11

EDITORIAL GUIDELINES AND CONVENTIONS

A: Script Organisation and Layout

1 Scripts are produced in units of modules, it **each module is saved as a separate Word document**. The documents should be named according to the module and its version: M01_V1.DOC.

2 Each document should be laid out with the following on the top of each page:
Working title of programme
Module number and title

3 Video shot notation: WS = wide shot, MS = mid shot, CU = close-up.
> means 'go to'.

4 Points of emphasis for the audio artists are indicated by <u>underlining</u> the word or phrase. 'sfx' indicates a sound effect.
Indicate any pauses required, other than the standard pause between audio files, which is one second.

5 Use **Times New Roman 12pt** throughout the script.

6 Footnote indicates: Document file name, Version number, Date, Page no.

B: Text

1 Full stops are to be used only between two sentences that follow straight on. **Single space** after full stops.

2 Avoid using semicolons. Use colons only where you have a heading and a point relating to it on the same line, eg **Aim: To go through the monthly sales figures**. Don't use a colon before a bulleted list unless the sense <u>absolutely</u> demands it.

3 Bulleted lists begin with a capital letter for each point.

C: Conventions

1 All **summary** text screens build in time with any audio.

2 Between each audio file there is a short pause of one second (unless otherwise specified by the writer).

3 At the end of a sequence, where the Menu or Forward button will be highlighted, leave one second after the last event (audio, text build or video clip), then activate the highlight.

4 With multiple-choice questions, the user's selection is indicated with a yellow highlight. The correct answer is subsequently indicated with a tick(s). The user's choice(s) remains highlighted when tick(s) appear.

    ☐ script or PRM format

    ☐ editorial guidelines and conventions.

- The general approach should provide a brief description of how text, audio, graphics, animation, video and interactions are to be used in relation to the TBT programme in question.

- The use of function and navigation buttons should detail which functions and buttons have to be included and how, where and when they will operate.

- The standards laid down for the style, tone and pitch of the text, audio, graphics and video need to relate to what is known about the target audience and its profile.

- Providing some guidelines and conventions for the use of both formative and summative assessment is a vital part of a briefing and specification document, because this aspect is often the weakest part of many TBT programmes.

- Precise guidelines and conventions should be provided for the production of the PRMs or scripts.

- Additional editorial guidelines and conventions will probably also have to be included to ensure the consistent production of scripts or PRMs.

6 Instructional Interaction

Introduction

Take a group of people, put them together in the same physical space, throw in a really good facilitator or trainer – and bingo, you have all the potential for loads of interactive learning. Alternatively, take one person complete with a computer, lob in a really well-designed TBT programme and you can achieve exactly the same result, particularly if the learning is online! Believe me, you can. The funny thing is that most people don't have a problem with expecting interaction to be a key feature of the first type of learning, but they often do with the second type. However, the fact is that both types of learning require an initial capability to be present – that of being able to provide interaction – but I suppose, because face-to-face learning is far more common and has a much longer history, plenty of interaction is both expected and taken for granted.

The very real and great danger with TBT is that if it doesn't embrace as fully as possible, as and where relevant, all the various forms of interaction available, then it will never realise its true potential and will ultimately become the poor relation of training delivery methods. This is where the art of the instructional designer really comes to the fore in being able to make the TBT programme as interactive as possible.

Take a look at these comments which were made by people after they experienced some TBT programmes:

■ 'Don't expect me to read page after page, with little or no interaction.'

■ 'Don't show me endless sequences of video shot 10 to 15 years ago, followed by a series of inane questions.'

■ 'Don't make me click and click and click to get to the part I want to look at.'

■ 'Give me a phone number of a real, live person so I can ask questions.'

Do any of these strike a chord with you? If they don't, then you can count yourself extremely lucky!

This chapter looks at the various types of interaction that can be built into TBT programmes and some of the main ways in which they can be used. Probably the most important thing to remember is that although there are many different ways in which to build interaction into a TBT programme, it is how the interaction is used and at what stage that is all-important.

Getting interactive

Now, there was a time when this form of TBT consisted mainly of screens and screens of text; the idea of a 'totally fulfilling interactive experience' was the ability to hit the space bar to move on. Amazingly, there are still some people today who think that it's perfectly acceptable to take some text, such as this book, convert it into an electronic format, and then call it TBT!

In Chapter 2 I outlined four different types of interaction: control, involvement, feedback and variety. Because of the historical and often painful experiences of many TBT users of yesteryear, it is important to stress just how varied interaction can be, and to illustrate all the various options available to instructional designers. I shall now look at each of these types of interaction in a little more detail.

Control

An element of control is inherent in most TBT programmes, particularly those that will be used at a distance, because users are able to control to a certain extent the pace at which they learn. However, this should not be the end of the story – just the beginning, the instructional designer thinking of all the other ways in which users could be given control in relation both to the learning objectives and the content of the TBT programme in question.

Table 16 on page 102 shows some of the ways in which user control can be built into a TBT programme and the means by which these can be achieved.

Although it may not be necessary to include all these control features in every TBT programme, each feature should be considered as a possibility in relation to the programme in question and in relation to what learning that programme is attempting to achieve.

Involvement

Another important aspect of interaction is to provide users with the opportunity to feel involved with what they are doing. Because most adults like to feel a degree of involvement when undertaking any form of learning, TBT should not be seen as something 'done to' someone; it is, rather, something with which they can get involved. In some ways, involvement is similar to control in terms of the ways a TBT programme can be used, although the means by which it can be achieved will be slightly different. Table 17 on page 103 shows some of the ways in which involvement can be included in a TBT programme.

Table 16

CONTROL

Ways	Means
Pace of learning	Make sure that the various assets used (audio, graphics, text and video) are not scripted so that they take place automatically over several frames, because this will mean that it is difficult for users to pace their learning.
Repeating parts	Provide users with the opportunity to go back to various modules, sections and so on by allowing them to revisit any parts of the programme as and when they want to.
Controlling audio and video	By using a video-type control panel, users can always pause the audio or video and start or stop it again whenever they wish – a very useful feature, particularly if you get interrupted or just want to pay a visit somewhere!
Next frame	One way of allowing users to move to the next frame when they want to is to have the forward button 'active' all the time. However, this is not always the most sensible thing to do if it's vital that all the contents of a frame are visited before moving on. In such cases it's important to make sure that, within reason, the content of frames is relatively short, so that users are provided with a reasonable degree of control and do not have to wait for ages until they get an opportunity to move on.
Going back or forward several frames	The ability to go back a few frames should be a built-in feature of all TBT programmes. The instructional designer should ensure that such opportunities are provided at regular intervals, encompassing a given number of frames, such as those that cover a specific learning point. The opportunity to advance a number of frames at a time should also be considered, particularly when users are revisiting parts of the programme. Here a button such as one used to fast-forward a video could be a regular feature.
Bookmarking a frame	Providing users with the opportunity to mark a frame so that they can revisit it at any time is a useful feature, although it does add to programming requirements.

Finding out more	Sometimes a frame can consist of a number of related aspects that are optional or can be 'visited' in any order users desire. The instructional designer has to consider whether this type of control is viable and, if so, provide it. Likewise, it may be desirable to provide some links to other parts of the programme so that users can find out more about a specific learning point.
Exit now	Although it may not seem like it, the opportunity to exit whenever users wish is a most important feature of controlling a TBT programme.
Returning after exit	If users have to restart a TBT programme from the very beginning or from the first frame of a particular module, they will probably not want to exit mid-way through a particular frame or sequence of frames. Therefore the ability to return after exiting to the frame where they left off is a vital control feature.

Table 17

INVOLVEMENT

Ways	Means
What to study and when	By providing a programme map, users can see what's available and how the whole programme hangs together. Pre-testing will also allow users to decide what parts of the programme they need to study; accompanying the results of the pre-tests with some tutorial advice could assist users in deciding when these various parts need to be looked at.
Study order	Sometimes it is feasible to allow users to study all the various parts of a TBT programme in any order they desire. Where this is possible, because each part of the programme is a discrete entity in its own right, users will automatically become involved in the training programme. In other situations where fewer choices are available (owing to the way in which the content has been structured and sequenced), it is still important to indicate to users just where they have control over the order in which they can look at the relevant parts.

(continued on page104)

| Diagrams and objects | Another way in which to get users involved with their learning is to allow them to interact with such things as diagrams and other objects. This can be achieved by letting users click on various parts of diagrams to see 'what might happen if...' or by allowing them to move different objects around or interact with them in some way. |
| One-to-one instruction | In many ways, using a TBT programme can be like having your own personal tutor on hand the whole time, albeit in electronic format. To encourage users' involvement, the style and tone of the audio and text can do a lot to 'personalise' the learning experience. In addition, the clever and creative use of providing detailed and specific feedback which suggests or recommends going to another part of the programme or undertaking a certain activity will also greatly enhance users' involvement. On top of this there is also the potential to involve users even further by building-in other forms of online tutorial support, which I shall cover later on in this chapter. |

Feedback

When people are in the process of learning, particularly when that learning is in the form of training, providing feedback in a variety of different ways will always prove to be invaluable. People like to know how well they are doing, to be able to get assistance as and when they need it and to be able to check up on how much they have learned. In a face-to-face learning environment and with a proficient tutor or facilitator there is plenty of scope for all manner of feedback. However, the same can be true for TBT, provided every opportunity is taken by the instructional designer to make it so. Table 18 shows some of the ways in which feedback can be provided and how this can be achieved.

Table 18

FEEDBACK

Ways	Means
On-screen help	Asking for help is a form of feedback – provided it is given, of course! On-screen help for users who get stuck may be provided in the form of technical assistance in using the TBT programme, or related to the subject matter in question or to additional tips and hints to assist users' learning or progress through the programme.
Questions and answers	Rather than just sitting there clicking on their mouse from time to time to move on to the next frame, users should be asked questions at sensible intervals which they are required to answer either by keyboard input or by selecting answers from a list supplied. In this way users have a chance to interact with the programme and to check on their progress at regular intervals.
General feedback	After each learning point or enabling objective has been covered, some feedback should provided. This means a question should be asked of users that requires some form of interaction, either by supplying or selecting an answer, or by clicking on or interacting in some way with an object.
Pre-tests	Another form of feedback is to allow users to undertake pre-tests or self-assessment quizzes so that they can check on how much they already know. This is important when it is known or it is likely that the target audience in question already possesses some of the knowledge and skills covered in the programme.
Post-tests	The ultimate form of feedback is to allow users to undertake post-tests or tests of mastery at key stages so that they can assess how much they have learned and to what extent they have mastered the terminal objectives. In this way it is also possible to provide them with advice on whether they need to study part of the programme again.

Variety

One of the benefits of interaction is to provide users with some variety and to get away from the feeling that all they are doing is to click, click and click again until they get to the end – at which point they can breathe a great sigh of relief! By breaking up the programme into discrete 'chunks' of learning, and by using different forms of stimuli that require some form of user interaction, variety is introduced – which usually serves to keep the user interested and wanting more. Table 19 shows the two main ways of adding variety to a TBT programme and the means by which interaction can be achieved.

Table 19

VARIETY

Ways	Means
Different stimuli	By using different forms of input (such as text, audio, video and graphics) and asking users to interact with each of these in different and appropriate ways, you can ensure that plenty of different types of interaction are included in a TBT programme.
Other learning material	Another way of including a variety of interactions is to build into a TBT programme the use of other learning materials, aids or information, such as workbooks, worksheets, handouts, data tables and calculations. To think of a TBT programme as a stand-alone method of learning is not always helpful or appropriate. For example, it may be necessary to ask users to print something out and fill it in, or to perform a calculation. Users might also need to be provided with a workbook in which they can record certain pieces of information or be given additional tasks to do. On top of all this the use of online interactions as described later in this chapter will also ensure an even greater variety of interaction.

Being interactive

Knowing what's available is one thing – using it appropriately is quite another. This is where the art of the instructional designer really does come to the fore. Having said that, there is still an important caveat: the need for the instructional designer always to take into account the programming implications of the interactions he or she requires. Theoretically, anything is possible, provided it is appropriate; however, an instructional designer should also be totally aware of the programming implications. Time and budgets can often be major constraining influences on the amount and type of interaction built into a TBT programme.

Fit for its purpose

One of the most important aspects of using any form of interaction is to make sure that it's truly fit for its purpose. There is no point whatsoever in an instructional designer thinking, 'Oh, there's been no interaction for quite a while. I'd better bung some in…Now, let's see…Yes, I'll pop in a question, even though they won't have really covered the learning point at this stage…'. As far as users are concerned, inappropriate interaction usually stands out like a sore thumb because they often find themselves thinking, 'Why on earth have I been asked to do this?'

> If you have used a TBT programme at some point, have you ever wondered about the appropriateness of anything you were asked to do? If so, can you pinpoint what you were asked to do and why you thought it was inappropriate?

The instructional designer should always question or check his or her use of any form of interaction, in order to make absolutely sure that it is appropriate to a given learning point or objective. I shall now take a look at some of the uses of interaction and how they can be employed appropriately.

Moving around

One of the most important ways of providing interaction is to allow users to move as easily and freely as possible around a TBT programme. Programmes designed in a restrictive and rigid manner can be extremely frustrating to be faced with, and users can easily lose interest and enthusiasm in what they are doing. As mentioned previously, the instructional designer should think very carefully about how users will be able to find their way around the TBT programme, and what facilities, in terms of menus and buttons, they will need to allow them to do this. It is also important to make sure that such facilities are available when needed, although this does not necessarily mean that all of them should be available all the time. For example, there may be some occasions when the instructional designer does not want the user to be able to move forward until a particular learning point has been covered.

Selecting material

Asking users to make a selection of some kind is a most useful way of getting them involved with a TBT programme. They may be able to select modules or sections of modules as and when they want to, or they may be given a choice of options within a frame. For example, an instructional designer may want to show three or four different video scenarios that do not have to appear in any specific sequence. In this case, why not let users decide the order in which they look at each of these sequences?

Another way of selecting material is to provide users with particular objects or tools, such as help, noticeboards, glossaries and tutorial assistance (as a talking-head facility) which they can select at any time they need. In such cases, however, it's important not to provide so many of these additional facilities that users become confused and bamboozled by all the choices they have. Each object or tool should have a place and a purpose, be easy to select and do its job properly.

Responding to questions

Asking users questions (just as a face-to-face trainer would do in order to establish understanding) to check up on any problems and to provide feedback can also be a feature of TBT programmes. Used judiciously, an audio voice-over or a text box can help users to take just a few moments to think about what they have learned and to decide whether they need any additional help, need to go back a few frames or are happy to move on. This type of question is particularly useful when a specific learning point which is quite difficult conceptually has been covered and the instructional designer feels that it would be helpful for users to think about the extent to which they have grasped it. However, it is important to use such a technique with care (otherwise it can become immensely irritating) and also to make sure that the style and tone of the questions are not in any way patronising.

There will also be occasions when the instructional designer wants to check on knowledge or skill acquisition in relation to a specific learning point or objective that will require the use of a direct question or an instruction to the user. Such questions or instructions are vital in order for users to obtain feedback on the extent to which they have mastered an enabling objective or have grasped a learning point. A variety of options is available here, which requires the instructional designer to know how to use various assessment items appropriately – such as multiple-choice, matching, true-false, demonstrating a particular action or series of actions, and so on.

Providing and responding to feedback

When a question or instruction is provided it is essential that some form of feedback is also provided. That said, it's vital too that the feedback is constructive and helpful.

Just telling a user 'Yes, that's right!' or, worse still, 'No, that's wrong!' is totally patronising in the first instance and totally unhelpful in the other. There is an art to providing feedback both in terms of *what* is said and *how* it is said. First of all, it's always helpful to reinforce why users are correct, just in case they got there with a bit of luck! Second, if they are wrong, then wherever possible they should be told why their response was inappropriate and what the correct response should have been. Third, the tone in which any feedback is provided should be positive and not at all condescending.

Providing feedback is one thing, but what is often missing in a lot of TBT programmes is suggestions to users on how they respond to the feedback they have received. For example, in relation to the response they have given it may be appropriate to recommend that they go back a few frames, go to an additional section that provides further tuition, undertake a specific task or activity, or contact their online tutor. This aspect of providing further assistance to users on how they should respond to feedback is likely to become even more important as TBT is designed to extend beyond its normal 'stand-alone' boundaries.

Finding out more

When designing a TBT programme it is sometimes necessary to provide a link to enable users to find out more about a learning point or content area. For example, it may be an optional link along the lines of 'If you want to find out more, then…', or such a link could be provided with some feedback after a question or instruction has been given. The instructional designer should always be thinking, 'Is there anything else they might need to know or be able to do; is there any other area of this programme I should refer them to?'

It should also be accepted that it will not always be possible to provide everything a user needs in the one TBT programme. As I have mentioned already, this means that the instructional designer should always consider what other options are available, such as referring to existing materials, other sources of information, asking suitably qualified people for advice and support, as well as the possibility of using any relevant TBT programmes that are also accessible.

The important message here is 'Don't be proud!' Be prepared to entertain the thought that there is nothing wrong in recommending at certain stages that users may find it useful to look up x, y or z. Such links will serve only to support and enhance the TBT programme even further.

Practising tasks

Another useful form of interaction is where the instructional designer asks the user to practise some tasks. These tasks can be wide and varied, such as repeating a recently learned process or procedure, or stopping the TBT programme in order to go away and try out something for themselves. The notion that a TBT programme has to be completed at one or several attempts should be dismissed. Sometimes it is necessary to allow users to go back and repeat a procedure or process and, at other times, it is desirable to encourage them to take stock, switch off their 'umbilical technological cord' and go and try out something for themselves before coming back.

Undertaking activities

Now here is where we really start to get interactive – big time! A good and creative instructional designer will be able to incorporate into a TBT programme opportunities for users to engage in various activities as befits the learning objectives and the subject matter. For example, as it's already been suggested, it may be a simple (or difficult) calculation, it may be some other form of question or instruction, or it may even be printing out a screen and then going away to work on it in some way.

The options are endless once an instructional designer thinks outside the TBT programme itself and entertains the possibility of suggesting an activity away from the computer. Of course, it goes without saying that the activity itself has to be relevant, achievable, realistic and something that enhances or extends the learning at the point at which it is introduced. It is also important for the instructional designer, when thinking about such an activity, to consider whether it is something that needs to be done in conjunction with other users or whether the users themselves might require some additional forms of support to be made available to them, such as access to an online tutor.

Online interaction

Essentially, there are two main types of online interaction that an instructional designer should consider. The first type is where users may need to interact with other users to discuss issues, assignments, problems etc. The second type is where users may benefit from some additional tutorial support in terms of completing the training package, asking for advice and guidance or seeking clarification of their understanding.

Although there is currently nothing to stop a user of a stand-alone TBT programme having access to tutorial support over the telephone (other than the inevitable resource issues, that is), the advent of online learning and e-learning has placed much more emphasis on providing this type of support by using the additional facilities that the Internet and intranets bring with them. I mentioned in Chapter 2 some of the possibilities that now exist – such as e-mail, chat rooms and computer conferencing facilities – and with which instructional designers should now be familiar. At the time of writing all these additional forms of online and e-learning support are very much in their infancy, but this does not mean that instructional designers can afford to perform something akin to a kamikaze ostrich-type act! The harsh reality is that all of these constitute another set of challenges to the future state of the art of instructional design.

User-to-user interaction

The instructional designer may decide in some situations that users should be given the opportunity to interact with other users online. Where the content or subject matter of a TBT programme is contentious or open to different interpretations, needs to be enriched by a number of different experiences or requires discussion or debate, then the opportunities for engaging in some form of learning intercourse will have to be provided along with the TBT programme itself.

A 'chat room' could be set up to allow users to communicate with other users – one-to-one or one-to-many – at the same time. These are text-based areas and can, if not facilitated in some way, end up a bit of a free-for-all. For example, someone may ask a question and then several people provide answers to it. All these answers arrive on the screen in a random order, so it can be very difficult to know who is answering what question. A better way of doing this, although more resource-dependent, is to have a facilitator present who can filter the questions and answers that are arriving, and then release them in the correct sequence to everyone taking part. In this way everyone knows who is 'talking' and in relation to what. Another way of doing this is to use an asynchronous bulletin-type board or conference room, where users can 'post' their questions or answers. Because this doesn't take place in real time (ie it's not 'synchronous'), it does mean that users will need to go online from time to time to see what postings there are and to reply as appropriate. Again, it is possible to get someone to put all the postings for a day together and then issue the combined result at the end of each day. This way users know that the day's 'briefing' should be available by a certain time, which makes the use of such a facility a lot easier.

Using these types of text-based online communication methods does require users to be conversant with using e-mail-type technologies in terms of access and in terms of what to say, how to say it and when to say it. If an instructional designer considers this type of facility important, then its provision will probably have to be accompanied by some 'rules of engagement' for the users, such as avoiding symbols that only an enlightened few will understand readily, being helpful while not being afraid to say what they think (everyone is entitled to their view), and to avoid sending overly long, verbose and intellectually specious messages in the form of densely packed blocks of text!

Another form of communication that is becoming more widely available as costs fall is that of audio or video conferencing, which can be used in conjunction with an organisation's intranet. Video conferencing does require a wide bandwidth – which means that the use of this technology is still relatively new as a means of providing learning support. Again, its use requires careful consideration and management because it is not like talking to one person at the end of a telephone or interacting with several people in the same physical space. However, if the facilities exist and there is a need for several users geographically far apart to have a discussion of some kind, then the instructional designer should consider whether this would be a viable way of achieving this requirement.

Online tutor interaction

The concept of online tutoring is, at long last, starting to come into its own. As learners, we all need varying degrees of support, and to think that any TBT programme, no matter how superbly designed, could ever be used unaided by everyone is to fly in the face of reality. Using the same sort of facilities as mentioned for user-to-user interaction, the provision of an online tutor is now a real possibility.

However, before any instructional designer thinks, 'Whoopee, great stuff!', he or she has to think about what this actually means in practice. First and foremost, it's not an excuse to take short cuts with the TBT programme itself. Providing an online tutor is a means of enriching a user's learning; it's *not* a substitute for inferior instructional design in the first place. Second, due consideration must be given to who is going to be the online tutor, and whether he or she has got the required skills and knowledge.

Although it makes complete sense to choose someone who has already had plenty of experience as a tutor – because he or she should be able to communicate effectively, be well organised, be able to manage groups of people and, above all, have empathy with learners – there are some other aspects of being an online tutor that should also be considered. A good online tutor will need to have specific people skills, communication skills, organisational skills, technical skills and learning management skills, as well as the flexibility and enthusiasm to undertake such a role. Table 20 on page 116 shows some of the additional aspects that an instructional designer has to consider when deciding whether he or she has suitable online tutor support available.

Now, all of this is very important stuff for the instructional designer to take into account before deciding that online tutoring is a real possibility and something they can build into their TBT programme. This type of interaction has considerable potential to enrich the user's experience of a TBT programme, but only if people with the appropriate skills and attributes are available in the first place.

Table 20

ONLINE TUTORING

Skills and attributes	Why?
People skills	If anything, being an online tutor requires even greater people skills than those required when dealing with people face to face. In most cases online tutors are unlikely to meet users in person, so they will need to be able to establish good rapport by sharing information about themselves that will replace what they would provide if they met the same people in person.
Communication skills	Communicating online, particularly in an asynchronous, text-based environment, means that tutors must be very clear and concise, so that messages are not misconstrued. Likewise they may need to be able to read between the lines of what users are saying to them, pinpointing perhaps when a message contains a covert plea for help.
Organisational skills	In a face-to-face environment it's obviously easy for a tutor to see who is there and whether or not they are taking part. Online tutoring is quite different, so the tutor has to be highly organised in keeping track of e-mails sent and received, in being aware of who is having problems, and in offering other means of communicating with users if e-mail is unavailable for whatever reason.
Technical skills	Online tutors must be proficient in the use of computers and associated software, especially Internet-based software. In particular, they must be able to use e-mail and associated features, such as computer conferencing systems, as well as to find and access various websites. Technical skills on their own, however, are not the whole story: it's also a matter of knowing when it is appropriate to use the tools available, ie when to use e-mail or facilitate a conference.
Learning management skills	Giving users the responsibility for managing their own learning is just fine and dandy if they can cope with it. Yet a lot of people, for a number of reasons, find self-managed learning far from easy, which is where online tutors have an important role to play. They may need to help users to work through a TBT programme, encouraging and motivating them. They may also need to facilitate online discussions and put learners in touch

	with other users. In other situations, online tutors may have to decide whether or not they are prepared to let some people 'lurk' in the background without making a contribution to a discussion. Sometimes it's better to let people 'lurk' for a while so that they can gauge the tone and direction of a discussion before getting involved. It is these types of decision that a good online tutor will make appropriately in order to help users manage their learning.
Flexibility and enthusiasm	In using online tutors instructional designers have to be confident that the tutors are flexible and enthusiastic people. Responding to users' needs online requires considerable flexibility. Online tutors do not have to be available 24 hours a day, seven days a week, but they do need to provide a consistent and regular service if users are to have confidence in the service they can provide. Online tutors should also show that they are enthusiastic about this way of learning, so that their users are also encouraged to persist with their learning.

In brief

- It's a complete fallacy to suppose that TBT programmes have no potential for including a lot of interaction – provided, that is, it's appropriate.

- The two things that can really distinguish a well-designed TBT programme from a poor one is the amount and type of interaction it contains.

- Interaction can be employed to give users control when using a TBT programme, to allow them to get involved with the programme, to provide them with feedback, and to furnish them with a variety of learning experiences.

- Although most types of interaction are possible, instructional designers should always bear in mind the amount of time and the cost of programming required to effect each of their preferences.

- Any form of interaction must be fit for its purpose: it should be seen as an integral part of the TBT programme, not just window-dressing!

▌ Interaction can be in the form of letting users move around a TBT programme easily. It can also allow them to select various aspects of the programme, objects or tools as they wish. Asking users questions from time to time is also another very useful way to initiate interaction, as is the provision of appropriate feedback, along with suggestions about what to do next.

▌ Another useful feature of TBT programmes is to provide users with links to other parts of the programme or to other appropriate resources. There may also be some occasions when it is appropriate to suggest to users that they stop the TBT programme and try something out for themselves before resuming where they left off. In a similar way, the instructional designer could also suggest that users undertake specific activities from time to time in order to assist or enhance their learning.

▌ Finally, there is now the option in certain circumstances to provide users with two main forms of online interaction: user-to-user or user-to-tutor. Things like e-mail, chat rooms and computer conferencing are all available for instructional designers to build into their TBT programmes when appropriate.

It's All in the Script

Introduction

It's in the technology-based training (TBT) programme
script that all the planning and thinking about instructional
design comes together. It's at this stage that the 'fun' really
starts, when the instructional designer or scriptwriter rolls
up his or her sleeves, gets a pile of cold wet towels at the
ready and engages his or her creative brain on full power.
The art of scriptwriting is a worthy and honourable
profession, and good scriptwriters should be treated with
due respect and consideration at all times if their output
is to be of the highest possible order.

Although producing the PRMs or scripts is the main thing,
the scripting process does not end there, because the scripts
have to be checked by subject-matter experts and others,
after which they will then need to be used again when the
TBT programme itself is alpha- and beta-tested. This
chapter looks at each of these stages in more detail and, in so
doing, attempts to provide some useful tips both for budding
scriptwriters and other training professionals alike.

Getting going

Although there are many ways in which scripts can be
produced, I am going to use the layout I described in
Chapter 5. As I said there, this layout has stood the test of
time not only for me but also for all those who, at one
time or another, have had the role of checking scripts and

who have been involved in testing the TBT programme that resulted. In order to demonstrate some of the key aspects of scripting I shall attempt to make these as realistic as possible by showing you a few worked examples of some extremely interesting – well, they may be to some! – subject matter.

However, before you find yourself in PRM land, just a word or two by way of an explanation about the examples I am going to show you. I have deliberately chosen an example based on financial services because, first of all, I am not a particularly great lover of numbers and, second, I always struggle to get my head around things like investments when they do not involve a simple calculation of compound interest! Because the complete programmed version of the PRMs you are about to see worked for me – yes, I experienced that eureka moment – I thought that some examples of the scripts themselves would be a really good way of showing just what can be achieved to help the numerically challenged understand some fairly important concepts.

Basic principles

Experienced scriptwriters vary in how they prefer to go about producing PRMs. Some like to script the audio first if this is going to be the dominant feature of the TBT programme; then they add the graphics, text, video and interactions so that the script is built up in the form of layers. Others prefer to visualise what the user will be experiencing and script as they go. I have to say that the latter is my preference, because I can then make sure that all the various assets are used appropriately and to their maximum effect. As far as I am concerned, scripting is a process of visualising what I am writing in terms of the real thing, and this is why I like the sort of script layout that I have suggested in this book, because it allows me to script in the way I prefer. The other good thing about this type of layout is that it is also easy for relative novices to TBT programming (such as subject-matter experts) to follow because it tells the story very clearly, albeit in some detail.

The other basic principle concerns the appropriate use of the various features that are at the scriptwriter's disposal and that were mentioned in Chapter 2. It is vital that all these features or assets should be used appropriately by the scriptwriter in order to ensure that users are able to learn to maximum effect.

> At this point you might like to take another look at the relevant part of Chapter 2, particularly if you feel a little hazy about the best use of all these features or assets.

Now, before moving on, another word of warning. The examples you are just about to see are just that – examples, and ones that I have chosen in order to illustrate certain points. They are not perfect – well, what is? – and it is also important to bear in mind that there is always more than one way to crack a nut! As the nut said to the hammer when the latter said, 'There's more than one way to crack you' – 'Yes, there is, but it all depends on what my instructional strategy is and what my briefing and specification document says!'

Starting up

The first frame of a module or section usually serves to introduce users to what it is about and what it is they are expected to do. Obviously this depends on the precise nature of the TBT programme in question, but the main thing is to set the scene, in order to get users off to a good start. Figure 12 on page 122 shows an example of how this can be done.

Figure 12

FIRST FRAME POSSIBILITIES

SECTION 6: UNIT-LINKED INVESTMENTS

Frame Number: 02.06.010

Instructions:
On entry

Graphic:
02.06.010a   Show Graphic 02.01.010a with all the captions except 'Unit-Linked Investments' faded down. As Audio T: 02.076.010a plays, metamorphose the caption into the animated icon for this section.

Audio T:
02.06.010a   In this section I am going to take you through unit-linked investments – one of the products commonly used by most financial institutions. When you have finished the section you should be able to: tell me what the main features of a unit-linked investment are, as well as describing what benefits they have for customers, plus explaining what limitations they have.

Instructions:
After Audio T: 02.06.010a has played, fade down Graphic: 02.06.010a and replace with Text: 02.06.010a.

Text:
02.06.010a   By the end of this section on unit-linked Investments you should be able to:
list the main features of a unit-linked investment
describe the benefits to a customer of a unit-linked investment
explain the limitations of a unit-linked investment

Audio T:
02.06.010b   To help you to master these objectives you will also need to be able to: calculate the value of a unit-linked investment fund over different periods of time to tell whether or not the value of a fund has grown in value, as well as being able to say what Pound Cost Averaging, Bid and Offer Price, and Bid Offer Spread all mean.

Text:
02.06.010b   *(add the following to Text: 02.06.010a in time with Audio T: 02.06.010b):*

Calculate the value of a unit-linked investment fund after a given period of time
Specify whether the value of the fund has grown in value
Define Pound Cost Averaging
Define Bid and Offer Price and Bid Offer Spread

Audio T:
02.06.010c   So, when you are ready, just click on 'Forward' to find out more about unit-linked mortgages.

Interaction:
If User clicks on 'Forward' > Frame 02.06.020.
If else:

Text:
02.06.010c   Just click on 'Forward' to move on.
When click on 'Forward' > Frame 02.06.020.

Here the scriptwriter has set the scene and has told users what they should be able to do by the time they have finished the section, as well as what they will need to be able to do as they work through the section. The audio has been used in a conversational style, the text performing a summarising and reinforcing role. Users are left to decide when they want to move on and are also provided with some help if they have a temporary mental aberration about what to do next! Both aural and visual stimuli are provided to complement and support one another, so that there is always something happening on the screen as the voice-over continues.

Moving off

Having started up, it is then a matter of moving on to the next stage. Figure 13 on page 124 shows something of what could take place.

Figure 13

WHAT NEXT?

Frame Number: 02.06.020

Instructions:
On entry

Graphic:
02.06.020a   Show Graphic 02.06.010a in its animated icon form and show
the animation in time with Audio T: 02.06.020a.

Audio T:
02.06.020a   A mortgage supported by a unit-linked policy works on basically
the same principles as an endowment mortgage, except for the
type of fund that is involved. A unit-linked investment is where
the performance of the investment is related directly to the price
of the investment fund. Typically, each month the investment
premium buys a number of units that will vary as their price
goes up or down. Here is an example of what I mean.

Text:
02.06.020a

Months	Premium	Unit Price	Number of Units Bought
1	£50	1.00	50.00
2	£50	1.05	47.61
3	£50	1.05	47.61
4	£50	1.10	45.45
			190.67

Instructions:
Display Text: 02.06.020a line by line. As last line with total appears, play Audio T:
02.06.020b. As Audio T: 02.06.020b plays, flash the related parts in Text: 02.06.020a
to highlight them and then show Text: 02.06.020b after Audio T: 02.07.010b has
finished playing.

Audio T:
02.06.020b   You should be able to see just how, after four months, the total
number of units is 190.67. This means that the value of the fund
is 190.67 times 1.10, which is £209.73p against the £200 of
premiums that have been paid. The fund has therefore grown in
value because the price of the units has risen.

Text:
02.06.020b   Total number of units = 190.67
Total premiums paid = £200
Value of fund is 190.67 x 1.10 = £209.73

Audio T:
02.06.020c   But what if the price then falls because of market conditions?

Instructions:
Display Text: 02.06.020a again and add Text: 02.06.020c line by line. As last line with total appears, play Audio T: 02.06.020d. As Audio T: 02.06.020d plays, flash the related parts in Text: 02.06.020c to highlight them and then show Text: 02.06.020d.

Text:
02.06.020c

5	£50	1.00	50.00
6	£50	0.90	55.55
7	£50	0.85	58.82
			355.04

Audio T:
02.06.020d   Now, after seven months the total number of units is 355.04. The value of the fund is therefore 355.04 times 0.85, which equals £301.78p, against a total of £350 of premiums paid. In other words, the fund is now worth less than the total number of premiums paid to date.

Text:
02.06.020d   Total number of units = 355.04
Total premiums paid = £350
Value of fund is 355.04 x 0.85 = £301.78

So, having set the scene in the previous frame, in this frame the scriptwriter really gets things moving by demonstrating and explaining how this type of investment fund works. Then, in line with the enabling objectives, users are taken through what happens when market conditions cause prices to fall, so that they should by now have the basic know-how. Notice also how the audio part has been written – in a style that is easy for the audio artist to read – and how the scriptwriter wants the text to appear in time with the audio.

What happens next? Well, here is how this particular writer scripted the rest of the frame.

Audio T:
02.06.020e   So, if the investment was cashed in after seven months there would be a loss. In this case, though, this isn't going to happen, so, with your help, let me show you what takes place over the next few months to this particular fund.

Instructions:
Display Text: 02.06.020c again and add Text: 02.06.020e with highlighted gaps that require input by the user. Make sure that the interactive calculator is active.

Text:

02.06.020e			
8	£50	1.00	50.00
9	£50	1.00	50.00
10	£50	1.10	
11	£50	1.10	
			_____

Audio T:
02.06.020f   Now have a go yourself at calculating the number of units for months 10 and 11, the total number of units purchased to date, and then work out the new value of the fund. Just type your figures in the missing gaps.

Text:
02.06.020f   Work out:
■ the number of units for months 10 and 11
■ the total number of units purchased to date
■ the new value of the fund
Press 'Enter' when you have finished.

Interaction:
If User types 45.45, 45.45, and 545.94 play Audio T: 02.06.020h followed by Audio T: 02.06.020i.
Audio T:
02.06.020h   Yes! Well done – that's quite right: 50 divided by 1.10. is 45.45 – give or take – and when you add up all the figures in the right-hand column they equal 545.94.

If otherwise, highlight incorrect entries and play Audio T: 02.06.020g:
Audio T:
02.06.020g   No, that's not quite right. Remember, you need to divide the premium by the unit price and then add up all the figures in the right-hand column. Have another go now at working this out. If you still get it wrong, don't worry, because I shall fill in the correct figures for you.

If still incorrect, fill in correct figures and play Audio T: 02.06.020i.

Audio T:
02.06.020i   Now, is the value of the fund greater than the value of the premiums paid? Click on the answer that you think is correct.

Instructions:
As Audio T: 02.06.020i plays display Text: 02.06.020g with two response boxes.

Text:
02.06.020g   Yes   No

Interaction:
If user clicks on 'Yes', play Audio T: 02.06.020j
Audio T:
02.06.020j   Good, well done. Yes, the fund is greater than the value of the premiums paid, because it is now worth £600.53p against the £500 worth of premiums that have been paid – which in any one's money means a profit!
> *Frame 02.06.030.*

If otherwise:
Audio T:
02.06.020k   No, the fund is worth £600.53p, against a total of £550 of premiums paid. This is because the value of the fund is 545.94 in terms of units bought, with a unit price of £1.10p, that is, it is 545.94 multiplied by 1.10 equals £600.53p.

Text:
02.06.020h   *(Show as Audio T: 02.06.020k plays)*
Value of fund = 545.94 of units bought
Unit price = £1.10
545.94 x 1.10 = £600.53.
Premiums paid £50 x 11 = £550

FRWD: > 02.06.030
BACK: > 02.06.020

Here the scriptwriter has decided that the time has come to ask users to show that they understand how the value of a fund is calculated. Because it had already been decided that the user interface would include an electronic calculator, just in case people wanted to use this instead of something else, the scriptwriter just mentions to the programmer that they need to check that it is available at this point. The audio tutor explains what he or she wants users to do, and then the instructions are presented as text, so that users can refer to them as they work.

The task having been performed, it's feedback time! Notice here how the feedback is given: positive, helpful and explaining why something is right and why something is wrong. The scriptwriter has also decided on this occasion that, after a second attempt, rather than make the poor old users go on *ad infinitum* until they get it right, it would be appropriate to fill in the correct answer for them. I suppose there are two reasons for this: one is probably that the calculation could easily be a few pence out (ie users' calculator skills may leave a bit to be desired!) so, although the users know what to do, their fingers and brain are not quite in unison; the second reason is that, because there will be other calculations later on, the scriptwriter doesn't want users to lose heart or patience at this point. Finally, the frame ends with another learning point in order to satisfy one of the enabling objectives, constructive and positive feedback once more being provided as appropriate. The script is now coming alive!

Gearing up

In the next frame the scriptwriter kicks things off with another calculation and appropriate feedback – again, filling in the answer if they get it wrong after a second attempt – and then moves on to another essential learning point. Figure 14 opposite shows how this was dealt with.

Figure 14

REVVING IT UP

Audio T:
02.06.030d   So, although the price per unit is the same as at the start of the contract, the value is now worth £833.92p as against £800 of premiums paid. This is because during months 13, 14 and 15 the unit price fell, allowing a greater number of cheaper units to be bought. Because of this the investment shows a profit, even though the fund price after 16 months is the same as it was at the beginning.

This outcome is known as Pound Cost Averaging, because the price of the units bought is equal to the average price during the life-time of the contract. In this way the main risk associated with buying a one-off, or single, premium investment is reduced.

Have a look at this graph, which shows how the unit price has risen and fallen during the 16 months.

Graphic:
02.06.030a   Graph showing the rise and fall of the unit price over time.

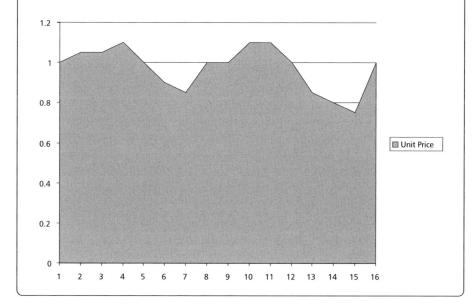

Audio T:
02.06.030e   Now, compare this with the graph that shows a linear rise in the premiums paid against a slightly fluctuating rise in the number of units bought, and a far greater fluctuation in the value of the fund over the 16 months.

Instructions:
Display Graphic: 02.06.030b under Graphic: 02.06.030a so a visual comparison of the two can be made

Graphic:
02.06.030b   Graph showing premiums paid, number of units bought and the value of the fund over 16 months.

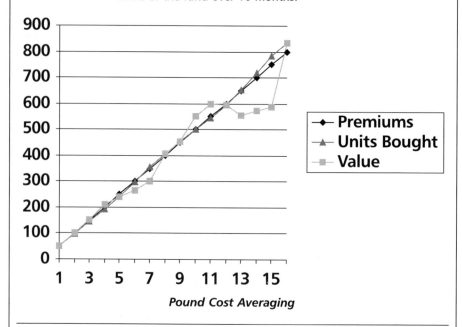

Pound Cost Averaging

Instructions:
Display Graphic: 02.06.030b by showing first the premiums paid, then the units bought, and then the value. The important thing is to show each component building up to illustrate the linear rise of premiums against the slightly fluctuating rise of unit against the greater and more obvious fluctuating rise of value.

Audio T:
02.06.030f   You should be able to see from these two graphs that it is the price at encashment that will have the greatest effect on the final value of the investment. If the price falls, then so does the value of the investment. However, although a low price can have its advantages during the purchasing period, because more units can be bought, at the end of this period it can be extremely disadvantageous! Remember those very sound words of advice? – 'The value of an investment can go down as well as up.'

So, although unit-linked mortgages are more volatile and risky than with-profit endowments, they can also produce higher returns at the end of the day. This is particularly so if borrowers can choose the time to encash their units.

Text:
02.06.030b   The price at encashment has the greatest effect on the final value
The last thing you want is to have a low unit price at the end
The value of an investment can go down as well as up
Unit-linked mortgages can have higher returns than with-profit endowments

FRWD: > 02.06.040
BACK: > 02.06.020

The scriptwriter has decided that it's now a matter of getting visual, and that the best way of getting over the concept of 'Pound Cost Averaging' is to do this with a couple of graphs, one of which needs to be animated – notice the instructions to the programmer and to the graphic designer here. The frame concludes by providing a text summary of the main points that have been made, after which users then decide when they want to move forward, or whether they want to go back and repeat the previous couple of frames.

Rounding off

There are many ways in which a section or a module can be rounded off and finished. Much will depend on what has been covered and how. However, two very useful techniques used by a number of scriptwriters, especially when difficult concepts have been introduced or several different learning points covered, is to provide some assessment test items to check on the mastery of the enabling or terminal objectives and, where appropriate, a brief summary of the module or section. Figure 15 shows you how this particular scriptwriter decided to round things off.

Figure 15

WELL, WHAT DO YOU KNOW?

Frame Number: 02.06.070

Instructions:
On entry

Graphic:
02.06.070a   Show Graphic 02.06.010a.

Audio:
02.06.070a   Now that you have had a good look at unit-linked mortgages, I would like to ask you some questions so that you can see how much you have taken on board. Just click on the answer of your choice.

Text:
02.06.070a   Which *one* of the following is the only guarantee with a unit-linked policy?
A. Assured basic sum
B. Sickness benefit
C. Set maturity date
D. Death benefit

Interactions:
Correct answer = 'D'.

If 'A':   No, the only guarantee is death benefit. The only insurance policy guaranteed to pay off the capital on a loan is a full, with-profit endowment, because the loan value is the same as the guaranteed sum assured.

If 'B':   No, the only guarantee is death benefit. Some 'mortgage protection' policies pay the lender interest on the loan if the individual claims on the sickness clause – but this is an extra policy, not the 'repayment' policy.

If 'C':   No, the only guarantee is death benefit, because a unit-linked policy could, in good investment market conditions, have sufficient value to repay the loan early, or it may need a longer time to reach the required value if market conditions are depressed. However, the life assurance element of the policy will cease at the notional termination date.

If 'D':   Yes, that's right. The only guarantee is death benefit.

Text:
02.06.070b   Which *one* of the following categories of investment has the highest level of risk?
A. Cash-based funds
B. Equities
C. Gilt-based funds
D. Property

Interactions:
Correct answer = 'B'.

If 'A':   No, the highest level of risk lies in investing in equities. Because the premium buys units, there is no underlying bonus structure or commitment to a guarantee that needs to be made. Provided the contract's minimum and maximum premiums are not excluded, there can be flexibility.

If 'B':   Yes, that's correct, the highest level of risk lies in investing in equities.

If 'C':   No, the highest level of risk lies in investing in equities. Unit-linked policy holders share in all the price movements, whether they are up or down. Because there are no reserves, when the underlying investments do well all the growth is expressed in the increased unit price.

If 'D':   No, the highest level of risk lies in investing in equities. Units can be purchased in different funds to match the investor's risk profile. The investor can switch funds and can also re-direct future premiums to different funds if they wish.

Audio T:
02.06.070b   That's the end of this section on unit-linked investments. Now choose where you want to go next.

Graphic:
02.06.070b   Show Graphic 02.01.030b with the Unit-Linked Endowment Mortgage option faded down and inactive.

Interaction:
If User clicks on Pre-Test > Frame 02.02.010.
If User clicks on Full Endowment Mortgage > Frame 02.03.010.
If User clicks on Low Cost Endowment Mortgage > Frame 02.04.010.
If User clicks on Low Cost, Low Start Endowment Mortgage > Frame 02.05.010.
If User clicks on Personal Equity Plan/Individual Savings Account Mortgages > Frame 02.07.010.
If User clicks on Personal Pension Linked Mortgages > Frame 02.08.010.
If User clicks on Post-Test > Frame 02.09.010.
If User clicks on Element 1 – Savings and Investment Products Module > Module 1c3 Frame 03.01.010.
If User clicks on Element 1 – Life Assurance Products > Module 1c4 Frame 04.01.010.

If otherwise:
Audio T:
02.06.000?   Just click on an item of your choice or click on 'Exit'.

Here the scriptwriter has opted to ask a few questions to check users' understanding of the various learning points and mastery of the learning objectives. This is probably a good decision, given what has been covered in this section! Because the learning objectives are concerned with knowledge and its application, the scriptwriter has opted for multiple-choice items. Although supply-type questions can always be asked, ie where users have to type in their answers, they make programming more difficult – for example, in making sure that spelling mistakes (unless these are not allowed for whatever reason) are taken into account. Select-type questions, such as multiple-choice and matching, are much easier to programme, although far more difficult to design.

Notice how the audio has been used to introduce users to the idea of a quick 'test' and to tell them what to do. Each multiple-choice test item is composed of a stem, the correct answer and three distracters. In each case, only one answer has to be selected, and this is quite clearly stated so that users are not left guessing as to whether there is more than one correct answer. The scriptwriter could have always decided to increase the number of distracters and ask users to select two answers, if appropriate. However, for each correct answer there should be at least three wrong, but plausible, answers or distracters.

Other features to note here are how the scriptwriter has made sure that the correct answer is not always in the same position, eg the second or third on the left, and that the list of possible answers is balanced in some way so that the correct answer does not stick out like a sore thumb! For example, in the first question the number of words in the possible answers goes three-two-three-two and, in the second question, three-one-three-one – no clues there, alas! Another feature that the scriptwriter has demonstrated here is a very useful form of feedback. Instead of telling users that they are wrong, they are not only told what the correct one should have been but also why their choice was wrong – nice one!

Finally, the scriptwriter tells users that they have now finished the section and asks the programmer to make sure that all the various links are in place, so that users aren't left high and dry, unable to move on. Umm – how does that all that feel? Not bad, I reckon, particularly considering the subject matter!

Inspection time!

Once the first draft of the PRMs or scripts has been completed, they need to be checked by the subject-matter expert(s) and the sponsor or client. This is an absolutely vital stage that should never be omitted, no matter how tempting it may seem at the time. By using a proprietary software word-processing programme it is relatively easy to supply the first draft to those who need it and to ask them to edit it as appropriate, using any revision facility by which each 'author' can be allocated a colour for their revisions. If time is short then 'authors' may have to work with scripts as they come off the production line. If time is not critical, then scripts can be passed from one 'author' to another so that each can look at the other's comments, and then a composite revised script can be passed back to the scriptwriter.

Every scriptwriter and project manager should accept that several drafts of the scripts may be required. When scripts are returned to the writer, that person has to take on board the comments received and then decide how to deal with them. This is not always easy, particularly when the 'authors' do not really understand the process of scripting, and, along with well-meaning comments and revisions, appear to have somewhat 'bastardised' the scriptwriter's work! It is therefore important at this stage for the scriptwriter to stand back and consider the value and importance of what the 'author' is saying, and then try to incorporate his or her comments in a way that does not have a negative impact on the overall instructional design or on the integrity of the script itself.

When the necessary revisions have been made, the scripts have to go back again to those who commented originally. Depending on the extent and nature of the changes and the stage the drafts have now reached, it may also be an appropriate time to let the graphic designers, programmers, and audio and video producers have a look at them as well, and to comment as appropriate. The whole idea behind this somewhat iterative exercise is ultimately to sign off all the scripts. Only when this has been achieved can the scripts be handed over to the production team, and the scriptwriter or writers take a short break before they are called into action once again.

Having a testing time

In my book – excuse the pun – the role of the scriptwriter or instructional designer does not cease once the scripts have been handed over to the production team. There is one last task to perform: helping to test what has been produced. If scriptwriters and instructional designers are not involved in the testing process, there is a considerable danger that the final product may not resemble the scripts on which it was based, in addition to the fact that all manner of undesirable things may have also crept in as a result!

The first stage of testing – usually called the 'alpha' stage – should involve both the instructional designer and the scriptwriters. They should work through the TBT programme alongside the scripts, noting errors or 'bugs' where the programme departs from the script and notifying the programmer if the former needs to be changed, or noting where the PRM itself needs to be changed because what happens in the programme actually works better! Sometimes the production team may have deliberately or inadvertently made things work or look better; if so, they should be credited with the fact. This stage is, therefore, very much a team effort, and it should be treated as such.

Once the comments of the scriptwriters or the instructional designer have been fed back to the programmers, another or 'beta' version of the TBT programme is usually produced. This version has also to be checked, only this time the client or sponsor should be involved, as well as a representative sample of the target audience (if possible). Once again the process is similar, all those involved logging errors or bugs along with those things that don't work so well and, in the case of scriptwriters or instructional designers, noting where changes need to be made to the programme or to the PRMs. In this way the final TBT programme and its accompanying scripts will be totally in accord. Believe you me, this is very important when it comes to making any future changes or amendments to the TBT programme!

Signing off (until the next time!)

Well, that's pretty much that for the instructional designer *cum* scriptwriter. Except, that is, for one thing, which is when the time comes for the TBT programme to be updated or changed in any way. Now this does depend to a certain extent on the nature of the changes required. If they are very small (for example, a change in something like interest rates, or an updated graphic showing a piece of equipment), and such changes do not have any effect whatsoever on the instructional design or integrity of the script, then the instructional designer does not really need to be involved. However, if any of the required changes affect the instructional design or the scripts in any way, the alterations will need to be checked first by an instructional designer and then the scripts amended accordingly. If this level of discipline is not present, the TBT programme and the scripts on which it is based are both likely to end up a chaotic mess.

So there you have it – the end of the scripting process has been reached. Although this process may appear to be a somewhat long and drawn-out affair, it's not really once it gets into full swing, and particularly when skilled and experienced instructional designers and scriptwriters are involved. Perhaps I am just a wee bit biased but, as far as I am concerned, the dear old scriptwriter is often the unsung hero of the whole enterprise. Programming is 'sexy', graphic design is dead creative, and audio/video production is just 'cool', whereas scriptwriting is, well, everything, because without the scriptwriter's art none of the rest would mean very much at all.

In brief

I Scriptwriting is the art of taking an instructional strategy and a briefing and specification document and making them come alive.

I Three stages are involved – producing the scripts, checking them and then using them to test the TBT programme.

I Where scriptwriters prefer and have the ability to do

so, the most effective and efficient way of producing scripts is to visualise what is being written in terms of the real thing.

∎ The other main determinant of a successful script is where all the assets, such as audio, text, graphics, video and interactions, are used appropriately and to their maximum effect.

∎ A script for a particular module or section of a TBT programme usually starts with an introduction of some sort that sets the scene, moves on to cover the first of a number of learning points, and then gets into full swing as more learning points and objectives are covered, before winding down and finishing off.

∎ Scripts should always be checked by subject-matter experts and the client or sponsor of the TBT programme before any further work is undertaken. This process requires time but it is an essential part of producing any TBT programme – leave it out at your peril!

∎ Most TBT programmes will need to be alpha- and beta-tested, a process in which the instructional designer or scriptwriter should play a key role. They should check the actual programme against the scripts, logging errors as they go. At the end of the testing, the PRMs and the TBT programme should be in total accord.

∎ The other role that should also be performed by an instructional designer or scriptwriter is checking and handling any changes or additions to the TBT programme where these affect the instructional design or the integrity of the scripts themselves.

Further Reading

DUGGLEBY J. *How to Be an Online Tutor*. Aldershot, Gower, 2000.

INGLIS A., LING P. *and* JOOSTEN V. *Delivering Digitally: Managing the transition to the knowledge media*. London, Kogan Page, 1999.

NEWBY T. *Cost-Effective Training: A manager's guide*. London, Kogan Page, 1992.

ROMISZOWSKI A. J. *Designing Instructional Systems*. London, Kogan Page, 1981.

ROMISZOWSKI A. J. *The Selection and Use of Instructional Media*. London, Kogan Page, 1988.

SLOMAN M. *The E-Learning Revolution*. London, Chartered Institute of Personnel and Development, 2001.

Index

systematic approach to 5–7, 8
see also technology-based training/learning (TBT);
    training
instructional strategy/strategies 41, 43, 53–76
    blueprint for/as *see* blueprint for/as instructional strategy
interactive TBT 15–17, 22, 28, 44, 83–7, 99–118
    options for 101–106, 108–117
    variety in 106
interactive video 9, 14, 16, 83
Internet, the 10, 11, 18–19, 21, 26, 28, 112–113
interpersonal skills, TBT and 22–3
intranets and extranets 10, 11, 18, 21, 26, 28, 112

LAN(s) *see* local area network
learning
    control of one's own 16
    effective methods of 3, 5, 6
    feedback following 5, 16, 44, 67, 90, 104–105,
        109–110
    in groups *see* group learning
    made easy 4–5
    methods for adults 2, 5, 8, 58–66
    one-to-one *see* one-to-one learning
    self-assessment following 17
    self-managed *see* self-managed learning
    support during/following 5, 17, 18–19
    transference of to performance in the workplace 2, 5, 7
    see also training; training programme
learning centres 18, 26
learning design *see* instructional design
learning difficulties, accommodating 38
learning environments 26, 39
learning needs of personnel
    identification of 1, 6, 22–3, 29, 31–2, 37–9, 40, 53
    in relation to organisational needs 3
    in relation to the disabled 38
    links to instructional design 2, 3, 8, 31, 37–9
    see also training needs analysis
learning objectives 7, 29, 31–4, 41, 52, 70

script format of/for 44, 49–50, 52, 72–6, 87–9, 91–6,
    119–138
style, pitch and tone of presentation of 44, 87–8
testing and validation of 44, 67–8, 70, 89–91, 136–7
user interface (the screen layout) for 44–9, 83–7,
    101–106
volatility (changeability) of subject content in 24, 29
text presentation, TBT and 13, 44, 83, 87
training (in general)
    access to resources for 39
    cost-effective solutions for 2, 8
    delivery of 1, 2, 5, 6, 7, 8, 70–72; *see also* media for
delivery of training
    design of *see* instructional design
    development of 1, 6, 7, 29
    effectiveness, assessment of *see* assessment of the
        effectiveness of training
    framework for *see* instructional design, systematic
        approach to
    needs *see* learning needs of personnel; training needs
        analysis
    objectives of *see* training objectives
    paper-based 10, 12
    programme for *see* training programme
    sequencing of 1, 5, 8, 33, 41, 57–9, 63–6
    strategy for *see* instructional strategy; learning objectives
    structuring of 1, 5, 6, 8, 33, 41, 57–9, 63–6
    technology in/for *see* technology-based training/
        learning (TBT)
training needs analysis (TNA) 7, 31–2, 46, 52, 55
    learning gaps 23, 29
    see also learning needs of personnel, identification of
training objectives (distinct from learning objectives) 7,
    31, 34, 54
    see also learning objectives
training programme 7, 54–70
    delivery of *see* training, delivery of
    design/redesign of *see* instructional design
    evaluating the effectiveness of *see* assessment of the
        effectiveness of training